Slab Huts to Commuter Country

A social history:
The lives of women in the Huon and Channel
(1900 to 2013)

W.L. Macdonald

Pikkeljig Press

First published in 2015

Pikkeljig Press
PO Box 388
Bayswater 6933 Australia

www.pikkeljig.com

ISBN-10: 0992511321
ISBN-13: 978-0-9925113-2-6

This study is dedicated to my friend and mentor Heather Jenkins.

"Lack of recognition of the part played by country women in rural life not only taxes their characteristic modesty and endurance but also obscures the ways in which rural communities and rural industry depend upon the contributions made by women." (James K. [Ed.] 1989: 2)

Contents

PREFACE   **I**

The author   i

The study   iii

Foreword   v

Acknowledgements   vii

Boundaries   ix

Inspiration for the study   xi

PART 1: 1900 TO 1945   **1**

Chapter 1: Introduction   **3**
1.1   Description of the study area   3
1.2   Purpose of the study   4
1.3   History of the area   5

Chapter 2: Family lives   **13**
2.1   Childhood   13
2.2   Provision of schooling   27
2.3 Education for the girls.   32
2.4 Adolescent years between school and marriage   37

Chapter 3: Home grown entertainment   **41**
3.1   The early years   41
3.2   Later in the century   42

Chapter 4: Life following marriage   **45**
4.1   Marriage   45
4.2   Motherhood   49
4.3   Community support   58
4.4   Women's suffrage   59

| 4.5 | Skill sets | 60 |

Chapter 5: "Modern" convenience — **63**

5.1	Running water on tap	63
5.2	Electricity	63
5.3	Motorised transport	66

Chapter 6: Working on the land — **69**

6.1	Farm and Orchard work	69
6.2	Alternative sources of income	72
6.3	Apple growing as an industry	74

Chapter 7: The effects of wars and the Depression — **79**

7.1	World War I	79
7.2	On the Home Front	82
7.3	After the war	83
7.4	The Great Depression	84

PART 2: 1945 TO 2013 — **95**

Chapter 8: The Post War period (1945-1967) — **97**

8.1	Slowly changing times	97
8.2	A childhood in the 1950s	101
8.3	Breaking the mould	102
8.4	A continuing way of life	103
8.5	Fashions change	103

Chapter 9: Natural disasters — **107**

9.1	Floods	107
9.2	Early bushfires	107
9.3	February 1967	110
9.4	Aftermath of the fires	122
9.5	In the Huon	123

Chapter 10: Life in the 1960s and 1970s — **127**

10.1	The decline of the apple industry	127
10.2	Career ambitions	129
10.3	Community change	129
10.4	Newcomers in the 1970s	130

Chapter 11: The years from 1980 to 2013   **133**

     11.1   The impact of change   133

     11.2   Childhood   134

     11.3   Education   135

     11.4   Entertainment and community life   137

     11.5   Marriage and motherhood   139

     11.6   Community support   141

     11.7   Technology in the twenty-first century   142

     11.8   Political awareness   143

     11.9   Working lives   144

Chapter 12: Conclusion   **147**

     12.1   Interview data collection   147

     12.2   Contrasting patterns   147

     12.3   Similarities between the lives of women in Part 1 of this study and the lives of women in Part 2 of this study   156

     12.4   Changes to leisure pursuits   157

     12.5   Changes within the communities   159

     12.6   Changes to technologies   162

     12.7   Changed political interests   163

     12.8   Summary of the study findings   165

REFERENCES AND APPENDICES   **169**

References   **171**

Appendix 1: Case Study participant information   **175**

     Introduction   175

     Additions to Case study 12, added after interview   175

     Case study: 60   176

     Case study: 61   178

     Case study: 62   179

     Case study: 63   181

     Case study: 64   182

     Case study: 65   184

     Case study: 66   185

     Case study: 67   186

     Case study: 68   187

     Case study: 69   189

Case study: 70   190
Case study: 71   190
Case study: 72   192
Case study: 73   193
Case study: 74   196
Case study: 75   197

Appendix 2: Women's war effort in World War I   **203**

Appendix 3: "Grandview" and Harry Sayer's homes prior to the fires   **205**

LIST OF TABLES

Table 1   51
Table 2   61
Table 3   108
Table 4   152
Table 5   157
Table 6   158
Table 7   160
Table 8   162
Table 9   164

Preface

View of Huon River Estuary. Photograph by the author

The author

I was born in Scotland and worked there as a teacher. My family came to live in Western Australia in 1981. My previous research has centred on social issues in education and I hold post-graduate degrees from Edith Cowan University and Curtin University in Western Australia. I have a long interest in the study of history.

In 2004 my family moved to live on the D'Entrecasteaux Channel in Southern Tasmania. I found, upon reading, that the local social history of the area focussed mainly upon the men who arrived from Europe and settled the districts of the Huon Valley and the D'Entrecasteaux coastline.

A general picture of the daily lives of the women who accompanied them and made their homes here over the years of the last century was lacking. Also lacking was a picture of the changes which have come about in the lifestyles of rural women in the area throughout the twentieth century.

It is this gap in knowledge that this study seeks to explore.

The study

The study focusses on the years 1900 to 2013. Data from the first sixty-seven years of the research has indicated settled patterns in the day-to-day lives of the women in the area. Many were born and lived within a small geographical area. Most married and worked alongside their husbands in family businesses, largely on rural orchard properties.

In the early years of European settlement before 1900 women, some of them convicts, lived isolated lives with their husbands who worked as timber fellers in the densely forested area. As land was cleared the families moved into farming and orchard growing. Towns and villages grew in the area. Communications improved. The pattern of the families' lives was then settled, though wars and Depression took their toll.

This settled way of life continued, relatively uninterrupted, through external difficulties, wars and the hazards of natural events until disastrous bush fires raged through the area. These fires particularly affected the Channel in 1967 and destroyed much of the countryside, costing sixty two lives in total.

The apple industry was already in decline due to over-expansion and to the difficulties of shipping to overseas markets. The destruction caused by the fires accelerated this decline and finally in the 1970s, with Britain joining the Common Market, a major overseas customer base for apples was destroyed. Many of the apple and pear orchards which had covered the land were pulled out, with Government blessing and compensation. Some farmers turned to raising sheep and cattle, while other properties were divided and sold off. This major change in lifestyle altered a way of life which had been in place for three or four generations of settlers.

As the twentieth century moved into its last decades a whole new set of circumstances arose. Travel to and from the State capital, Hobart, was now easy. New comers with property in the Valley and on the Channel could work in the city and return home each evening.

New industries grew in viticulture and cherry orchards. Small farm lots provided organic crops for niche markets.

Higher education for women had become established and University degrees were more common. Professional careers were pursued and the role of wife, mother and co-worker on the farm or orchard changed to that of, for example, doctor, teacher, architect, nurse or scientist, married or not married, with or without children but combining many roles while still seeking to enjoy a rural lifestyle. The women of the Huon and Channel would still be classified as living rural lives, but these lives now are a far cry from conditions in place around 1900.

Foreword

When I decided to conduct this research I started by using the convention of the third person as writer: "the author" or "the researcher". I have come to the conclusion that this format is too stilted and impersonal to accomplish the task I have set myself.

My intentions in writing this report were and are to present a picture of the lives which were lived by a number of women in the Huon and Channel throughout the twentieth century and into the early years of the twenty first century. If this attempt is successful then it should be accessible to a general readership and not solely the province of academia.

For this reason I will write the stories of the women and acknowledge my place amongst them by using the personal pronoun "I" when alluding to the author.

Acknowledgements

It would have been impossible to write this book if I had not been able to access the work of earlier historians. Without the work of Madge Lowe, the stories of the wider Channel area might well have been lost. I gratefully acknowledge Madge's help and advice. Historical detail has been collected and published by Julie Gardam. I am grateful for her permission to draw upon her work.

In the Huon area two sources have been particularly helpful. Oral histories were documented by Watson, 1987 in "Full and Plenty" and the collection of mini-biographies which forms "Heroes of the Huon" was edited by David Hammond. While stories of women's lives were in a minority in these publications I am grateful to the authors who carried out this work and to the organisation which published "Heroes of the Huon". I also acknowledge those who have published biographies and autobiographies for the detailed descriptions in these works.

The help given to me by Cygnet Living History Museum, the South Channel Progress Association, The Apple Industry Museum at Grove, the Glen Huon History Group and the Channel Heritage Museum has been invaluable.

In particular I would wish to thank the librarians at the Cygnet branch of LINC for their unfailing patience, for their advice and for the time they have taken to listen to my efforts in explaining what I have needed and what I have been trying to do. Without their help I would have given up the project.

My thanks must be extended in particular to the women who were prepared to share their personal stories with me in interviews. In writing this book I made an early decision to use a case-study format. By this means I could protect the privacy of the women whose stories were being told. Their names are not included in the text. I gratefully acknowledge the help and encouragement of these women and insights their stories have provided. I acknowledge those who have shared family photographs with me and given me permission to use these, especially Steve Lucas for the use of his extensive collection of family photographs .

I am grateful to Callum Macdonald, Jim and Miriam Birch for

technical support to back up my limited computer skills. Most importantly, I acknowledge the support and encouragement of my husband who has helped me throughout this study.

A special thank you must go to Dan Djurdjevic, of Pikkeljig Press, for all his patient work and expertise in transforming an amateurish draft copy into a book ready for publication.

Boundaries

The research takes the form of 75 Case studies. This format means that most of the information is taken from the stories of the women of the Huon and Channel as told to oral historians and in biographies. In the later stage of the research, information was given to me in participant interviews and as answers to written questions. Each story contributed another piece to an overall picture of life for women in the Huon and Channel. As with any oral history, however, data is dependent on what the participant choses to reveal. There will be gaps.

In the early case studies, moreover, there is no record of what questions were put to participants. Their stories were recorded or submitted to the author in written form and then assembled into print, arranged by the district in which the participant lived (Lowe undated and 1994: Watson. 1987). In "Heroes of the Huon" (Hammond (Ed.) 2004) the stories were researched and written by contributing historians. In three case-studies the stories are taken from either autobiographies or biographies (Tinning 1947: O' Rourke 2008: O'Malley 2009). The lack of structure of data gives many varied accounts of life in different areas of the Huon and Channel but in its raw form is not amenable to analysis. By taking each story as a case-study and analysing across the data I was able to identify emergent themes and to see where stories echoed each other, or were contradictory, across aspects of the women's lives.

Later interview data, which I have collected, was based upon a series of written questions which dealt with information gathered from the earlier histories. The participants in this part of the study were reached through personal contact, through introductions from friends and, in one case, as a response to a published request for information. The only two selection processes I applied were attempts to find a spread of stories from all parts of the Huon and Channel district and to find participants in a range of age groups from around thirty years old to eighty plus years old.

Because the responses in Part 2 of the study were governed largely by the questions posed, analysis was simpler. However, no attempt was made to limit responses to the parameters of the questions and many valuable insights were gained from wider ranging discussions instigated by the participants.

Despite examining 75 case studies, I make no claim that the information I have gathered is representative of all the lives of the many women who call, or have called, the Huon and Channel their home. Rather, I hope that I have painted a general picture which records some of the social history of this area of Southern Tasmania.

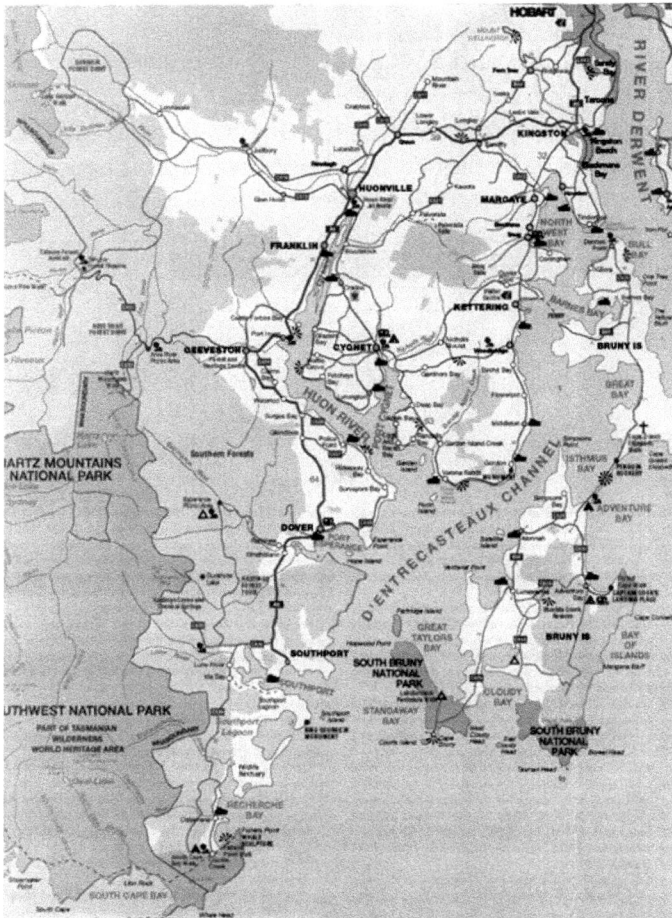

Map of the study area within its Tasmanian context

Inspiration for the study

When I first considered working on this research I was inspired by an oral history project, the results of which had been published in Scotland in 2008. The project had been carried out by a team of researchers directed by Dr. Mary Young, a local historian, and dealt with the history of a small parish near to where I was born.

"Abernyte" commences with a poem dealing with a local experience during the Second World War. It seems fitting to begin this book with a poem written by a woman from the Huon and Channel. I met Rose Webster in a café in Cygnet early in 2012, when this study was at a starting point. We got to chatting over lunch and I explained what I was doing. Her interest lay in the history of the Glen Huon School and she had written a paper about this. I had hoped to have an opportunity to talk further, but her health was poor over last winter and, although I have tried to contact her by telephone more recently I have been unsuccessful.

At our meeting in Cygnet, however, she wrote on the back of a menu a poem she had composed entitled "Walk in History". She gave me the hand-written, signed copy and permission to use the poem if I could. Here it is.

Walk in History

Some day we may find out why
Some stay low while some fly high
And we will better neighbours be
While we walk in history

Who can say why sorrows come
Why a mother leaves her home
Thinking she'll be better free
To walk alone in history

Can we take another's hand?
To show that we can understand
And walk a mile or two with him
Before his light of hope grows dim

It will not count for very much
If we have lost the common touch
Whatever we may rise to be
As we walk in history

Rose Webster (2012)

The sentiments in the poem seem to me to epitomise the strong sense of community and neighbourly-ness which shines through so many of the stories I have read and have heard in the course of this research.

Part 1: 1900 to 1945

Mountains between Huonville and Hobart. Photograph by the author

Chapter 1: Introduction

1.1 Description of the study area

In terms of natural beauty the Huon Valley and the D'Entrecasteaux Channel area of southern Tasmania is spectacular. Great mountains define the skyline. On their lower slopes, even today, areas of thick afforestation reach down to the shoreline beaches. Rivers rush down from the mountain plains to the sea. Where the forest has been cleared, pastureland and orchards fill the landscape, a landscape dotted with small towns and villages.

In the first years of the new millennium, the population of the Huon Valley according to census data stands at 15,140. This study, however, does not include the sparsely populated areas south of Geeveston. Kingborough has a population of 34,000, but the major population centres of Kingston and Blackmans Bay are outside the study area. The population of the area included in this book would be less by several thousands.

In global terms the area of the Huon and Channel is nearly as far south as human habitation reaches. The remoteness of the island of Tasmania was the reason it was chosen by the British Empire as a penal colony.

These districts have a long history of Aboriginal habitation. Early records tell of meetings between the French explorers who came to survey the coast and of the native tribes who greeted them. Because of the nature of Aboriginal culture, the story of these lost centuries only can be read by those who understand the significance of the shell middens and the stone tools and artefacts which survive. There are no written records prior to European settlement.

Sadly, later settlers clashed with the indigenous peoples as the incomers encroached upon traditional lands. Post-settlement, the stories of Aboriginal women and their treatment at the hands of the colonists from Europe make harrowing reading (Gardam 2005:

Townsley 1991, 32: Woolley & Smith 2004, 19).

Nowadays the capital of the State, Hobart, is within one or two hour's journey from the farthest part of the Valley and the Channel. Travel in and out of Hobart on a daily basis is commonplace. It has not always been so. At the end of the nineteenth century, walking over the high passes to Hobart could take days. With the advent of the stage coach the journey was one of eight hours (www.huonvalley.net.au). The Huon Valley is bounded to the north by the Mount Wellington Range, with the peaks of Sleeping Beauty dominating the skyline.

Transport by land was a near insuperable problem in the early days of settlement and difficult even until recent times. Barges rigged with gaff sails and, later, steamers from the Huon and Port Cygnet provided the most reliable form of communication with Hobart and the outside world. At one stage there were seventy major jetties on the Huon River (Hammond 2004, 15).

The land on the edge of the D'Entrecasteaux Channel, separated from the Valley by the forest-covered heights of the Snug Tiers, was serviced by those steamers as, again, there were few land routes to the north. In the near past roads have been improved and motor cars now make the journey relatively simple, though the roads still hug the coastline on the lower Channel and echo the earlier cart tracks.

1.2 Purpose of the study

This book sets out to tell the story of some of the women who have lived in the district from the early years of the twentieth century to almost the present day. These stories are told through 75 case-studies. Not all of these case-studies give extensive data concerning the lives of individual women. The aim of this book is rather to "paint" a comprehensive picture. Each detail of the case-study data contributes in some measure either to the overall picture, adds to that picture, or reinforces the image which is emerging. The women in the study are, in the great majority of cases, of European descent.

1.3 History of the area

"First—a bush house with ground for a floor had to be built....such accommodation was decidedly rough for a lady with three daughters accustomed to a civilised life—but the ventilation was first class." (Woolley & Smith 2004:119)

By 1900 most Aboriginal people in the area had been killed, had been moved elsewhere or had died from diseases brought with settlement. There were survivors, however. One of the most notable, especially in the area around Cygnet in the Huon, was a woman known as Fanny Cochrane Smith. Fanny Cochrane Smith was born on Flinders Island around 1834 and had married an English settler, originally from Kent in England.

Fanny Cochrane Smith, her husband and a group from the church. Photograph in the possession of one of her descendants.

William Smith had been transported to Tasmania and endured the horrific privations that were the lot of many convicts. He eventually worked at Oyster Cove and there was reputed to have seen a beautiful young aboriginal girl running on the beach. He fell in love with her and they married.

The Government of the day, in an act of reparation, granted Fanny Cochrane Smith land at Nicholls Rivulet (then known as Irish Town) and the couple made their home there. They raised eleven children. Mrs. Smith was widely known for her gracious hospitality to all those who lived near. The couple built a house with a room in it which was large enough to house church services. They were both staunch Methodists and were instrumental in having a Methodist Church built at Nicholls Rivulet.

Descendants of Mr. and Mrs. Smith still live in the vicinity of Nicholls Rivulet. One woman whom I interviewed for this project is the great-great-granddaughter of the couple and this photograph was given to me with her permission to use it as part of the study. Robyn Friend, who edited the book "We who are not here" in 1992, comments that there was at that time at least, a prevalent myth that all Tasmanian Aboriginal people died in the years following European settlement (Friend 1992: ix). Her book, a collection of Aboriginal oral histories rebuts this myth. That the myth is demonstrably untrue is proven by the presence in our communities of those who can trace their ancestry back to women like Fanny Cochrane Smith.

Tasmania, because of its remote location, was a convict destination for many who had fallen foul of the law in the United Kingdom. The European women who lived in the valley or on the Channel coast by 1900 were descended from convicts or from free settlers. These families had purchased, or had been granted, land. In addition to small farms, the men made a living from felling timber from the heavily forested countryside. As the forests were cut down, the cleared land was cultivated to provide the means for subsistence living.

Early living conditions were primitive. Shelter was provided by small huts built of the outer bark slabs of the felled timber. The roof was formed from cut wooden shingles. The bark slabs left gaps in the wall construction, through which wind and rain could penetrate the interior. To counteract this, the women would line the walls with scrim material over which they would paste newspapers. This laborious process produced a draught free and clean looking effect. The floors might be simple trampled earth, or might have wooden boards to provide cover. (Fenton: In Hammond 2004: 64: Lowe 1994: 49: Woolley and Smith 2004: 70)

Cooking was done on open fires and water was fetched from streams (Lowe 1993:16. Watson 1987. Woolley & Smith 2004). The huts might be set in isolated clearings in the forest, or might cluster round points where there was access to shipping such as at Port Cygnet.

These clusters formed the first basis for settlements, at Geeveston, Franklin, Victoria (later Huonville), Port Cygnet and on the Channel coast at Three Hut Point and Middleton, Peppermint Bay, the Oyster Coves, The Snug and North West Bay. Lady Jane Franklin, wife of the Governor of Tasmania became interested in the Huon area and visited the women with her stepdaughter Eleanor Franklin in 1838. Eleanor commented on Port Cygnet.

> *"Went to see all the huts in the place......We were very glad to see the great neatness of all the huts & of the women and & children. The huts all consisted of bark." (Woolley and Smith 2004: 67).*

Because of the patronage of Lady Franklin, land was occupied and settlements became established. By 1900 the population of the area was growing as the apple and pear industry thrived.

The settlements of Geeveston, Franklin, Huonville and Port Cygnet, along with smaller communities around the area, formed the nucleus of the population in the Huon Valley. The soil and climate were proving suitable·for the growing of berry crops and for orchards of apples and pears. Pastureland supported cows for milk, pigs foraged around the dwellings and hens were kept for their eggs. On the Channel coast fishing supplemented the food sourced from farming, orchards and timber felling, while boat building, fishing and scallop splitting provided other avenues of employment. (Lowe 1994: 65.: Gardam undated: 63. Perrin & Hay 1987)

Early records of the lives of women emphasise the focus on home and neighbourhood (Woolley 2002). Neighbours who gave support with work on the land were a valuable resource, as were the offspring of large families (O'Rourke 2008). A family might easily comprise ten children. Especially in the years soon after settlement, disaster was only a heartbeat away, whether through fire, flood or accident.

The huts all consisted of bark" (Woolley & Smith 2004: 67)

Life was hard and uncertain but food was not scarce, though intensive labour was required to secure this. Work on the properties could begin before daylight, with cows milked by the light of lanterns. The tasks might still be on hand late into the evening, packing apples in the sheds after children had been put to sleep. The land between the rows of trees was kept ploughed and clear, using horse drawn ploughs and sledges; berry fields needed constant hoeing, pigs were bred for slaughter. This task completed, the family tin bath might be used to clean the animal before butchering (Gardam undated).

Transport was still primarily by sea, with sailing ships supplanted by steamers. Stagecoaches provided a means of land transport but the journeys were long and hard. A coach leaving Geeveston early in the morning would reach Hobart by nightfall.

Not until the 1920s, when motor vehicles made an appearance on the roads of the Channel and the Huon Valley did conditions begin to improve. This and the eventual connection to the electricity supply did provide some relief from the physical demands made upon those who lived on the land.

The year 1914 saw the outbreak of war in Europe. Many young men from the Huon and Channel enlisted in what was supposed to be a great adventure. The absence these young men threw the burden of farm work onto those who remained. The loss of lives blighted the communities.

When the servicemen who survived returned, life went back to something resembling normal for a brief time. Then the world plunged into the Great Depression and the effects of this catastrophe were felt in the remote reaches of Southern Tasmania (Lowe 1993. O'Rourke 2008. Watson 1987). Markets for crops failed and the menfolk were forced to look for work away from their farms. This downturn had scarcely ended when another war loomed in Europe and once again the demands made on the womenfolk brought change to their lives.

This war was followed by a brief respite when the orchards prospered and the berry fruits provided good crops. In 1967, however, disaster struck the Huon and Channel communities in the form of terrible bushfires which destroyed homes, farms and orchards and took sixty two lives in Tasmania.

This catastrophic day spelt the end for many aspects of Channel life. Families who had struggled through the hardships of war and the Depression now were homeless, with orchards burned to cinders and cattle and livestock dead. Livelihoods were gone and families were forced to leave the district to look for work. The once thriving communities of the lower Channel became pale shadows of their former selves.

Then the main market for the apple crop, Britain, joined the European Common Market and that outlet for the fruit closed. These happenings, following hard on the bushfire catastrophe, drove many orchardists out of the industry. In the 1970s the Government gave money to have orchards pulled out (Gardam 2007, Lowe 1994, Watson 1987).

In more recent years a measure of prosperity has returned. Farms which were broken up and subdivided have seen new residents arrive to build hobby farms, to develop organic farming methods and to convert the fields that once grew berry crops into vineyards. Tourism ventures have sprung up and cars, each day, stream up the winding roads to Hobart carrying commuting workers.

The Mail Coach from Hobart to the Huon around 1880. (Huon Newspaper Co. Pty. Ltd. 17/12/36)

The Valley and the Channel communities have changed dramatically through the past century. Contributing to those changes have been the diversified roles of the communities' womenfolk.

It is true to say that local systems do not exist in isolation (Dempsey 1992: 251). These systems are integral parts of wider society, influenced by the structures and the ideas and values of that society. Therefore, aspects of life in the Huon and Channel will reflect the mores, cultural history, economic situation and the values of the wider society in Tasmania and indeed in Australia. However, "Nowhere is quite the same as anywhere else, even when subjected to the same influences." (Young 2008: 10).

In the case of the Huon and Channel in the early years, the

remoteness of the location may have restricted the influences from external sources. The communities, which developed in the Huon Valley and the Channel in the early years of the twentieth century, formed close- knit bonds of family and society. The small townships, from Margate (originally known as North West Bay) in the north of the Channel, through the tiny communities of Sandfly, Kaoota, and Pelverata in the pass between the Channel and the Valley, to Huonville, Franklin and down to the Hartz Mountains and Geeveston were founded and grew in isolation. The same was true in Snug, Kettering, Woodbridge , Middleton and Gordon on the Channel and in Port Cygnet back in the Valley.

The women whose families settled these areas relied on each other for help, support and companionship. In order to map the course of change in the lives and roles of women in the district throughout the twentieth century and beyond, it is necessary to start the journey with the lives and experiences of these earlier pioneers.

In the present day influences from the wider world are all-pervasive. Working lives can be spent in the city. Mass communication brings pictures of distant wars into the living rooms of each home. Journeys which once took days can be accomplished in less than an hour. Travel overseas is commonplace. Yet small areas retain their history and elements of an earlier culture and seek to preserve these. This book sets out to examine the lives of some of the women of the Huon and Channel, who experienced changed demographic structures, changes in education, wealth and lifestyle over the last century.

Chapter 2: Family lives

2.1 Childhood

"It was lovely living in a big family." (Watson 1987: 52).

Of the fifty nine women whose stories make up the content of this part of the research, thirty one told oral historians that they were born in the Huon Valley or on the Channel. Ten were definitely born outside the area of the study and moved to the Huon or Channel with their families. Oral history information does not specify where the remainder of the women were born.

For many, their families had come to the south as the descendants of the earliest settlers. Some had family members who were transported as convicts to Tasmania. In one case in Part 2 of the study the family had direct descent from a surviving member of the Aboriginal people of the south of the island.

By the year 1900, living conditions had improved for most. The bark huts of the original homesteads had, in many cases, been replaced by more substantial dwellings. No longer was it necessary in most cases to cover the inner walls with scrim and newspaper to keep out wind and rain, although for at least three families the privations of country living contrasted with former comforts.

The woman in Case 43 moved with her family from Bellerive, across the Derwent from Hobart, to an orchard property in Sandfly in 1935. They went from a town house with an inside bathroom and toilet to a home set in thick bush.

There was no electricity, so they had to use oil lamps and candles. Water was boiled on the woodstove to fill the tin bath in front of the house. The toilet was outside and well away from the house. They had to walk three miles to Longley to catch a bus to Hobart (Lowe 1993: 16).

In Case 2, the woman whose history is told moved with her

husband from the relative civilisation of the Franklin area to a bush dwelling nine miles up-country from Judbury. Her home there was so small that the couple's daughters slept in a tent in the garden. She cared for this property with the help of her children as her husband went prospecting for tin and felling timber. (Fenton. In Hammond 2004: 64)

Another family moved to the Channel from England (Case 42). The house this family came to in the Channel was built of weatherboards with a red iron roof and it had a dormer window. There was a front veranda and a central hallway.

To the right was a drawing room (not very large) which they furnished with a piano and various family pieces brought from England and a carpet bought at the Bath and West of England Agricultural Show. The girls had stained the surrounding floorboards with permanganate of potash crystals and then brushed them with linseed oil.

The girls slept in two rooms to the left of the passage. The contrast in size of the rooms to their home in England is noted, as is the fact that gas lighting and central heating were available in England but not in their new home (Tinning 1977: 19/20).

Where new homes were built, they were still constructed from timber in most instances as this material was freely available. The houses were larger, some with porches or verandas like the one described above, but still modest in comparison to the stone built mansions of the wealthier families of the areas north of the Huon and Channel. Most were built by the men of the family as they acquired land and set about cultivating this.

A typical house in the early years in Franklin might have four rooms, with a lean-to kitchen and a veranda. Until laths and plaster became available the walls were still covered with hessian and then wallpaper. As the family grew more rooms would be added to the structure (Lowe 1994: 49).

The photograph taken by the author with permission from the present owner of
the property.

The photograph above shows a family home built in the early years
of the twentieth century at Flowerpot on the Channel. The property
was the centre for orchard growing along with berry fields.

While still of wooden construction the building has advanced far
beyond the simple wooden shack of earlier times. A pleasing veranda
would provide a place to sit on summer evenings and the sheltered
porch protects the front door.

In the background are the densely forested hills of the Snug Tiers.

The present owners gave permission for this photograph to be
taken and were kind enough to allow me to see the interior which
retains walls panelled with pressed tin.

The photograph on the next page shows a reconstruction of a
kitchen interior from the early years of the twentieth century. This
family could obviously afford a more sophisticated cooking range
rather than cook over an open fire.

Photograph by the author from the collection at the "Apple Museum" at Grove in the Huon Valley. Taken with permission 10/07/2012.

As the exhibit demonstrates, the amount of work required to manage kitchens would have been substantial. The cast iron range would, in itself, take cleaning and maintenance. The firebox would require daily emptying. Looking at the largest of the cast iron kettles it is easy to see that, even empty, it would weigh a considerable amount. The bellows hanging by the fire would have to be worked encourage the fuel to burn, fuel which would have to be chopped and carried into the house.

The bread on the table would be freshly baked, probably each day. The eggs would be collected from the poultry which roamed the property. The milk would come from the family cow and the butter and cream would be churned or separated in the dairy.

More spacious these homes may have been but, in the early years, by modern standards, facilities were primitive. As with the family from Bellerive, there was, of course, no electric power. For the women, work in the house was carried out by the light of lamps and candles. Cooking was done over open fires or on wood stoves.

There were no bathrooms or toilets in the dwelling and no running water. A pit toilet could be a distance from the house.

Sanitation was primitive. The toilet outhouse was built away from the dwelling and a long, dark, cold walk was necessary to reach it on a Tasmanian winter night (O'Malley 2009).

Baths were taken in a tin tub placed in front of the fire and filled with water from the copper. The whole family would bathe there. As late as the 1950s, one woman I interviewed (Case 69) has described how the whole family bathed in a galvanised tub, five feet long by two feet deep. Baths were taken on a Sunday night in front of the fire with kerosene tins filled with hot water heating on the hob. The youngest of the family would be bathed first, with sometimes two or three little ones sharing the tub. As the water cooled, hot water from the kerosene tins would be added for the last lot of bathers.

In those conditions, the women of this period were raised in what, nowadays, would be considered large families. Ten of those who told their stories stated that they were one of six or more siblings. Most enjoyed being part of a large family with the companionship of brothers and sisters.

For those women, then, the training for the lifestyle which they were to follow began when they were very young. Sixteen of the women whose stories are recorded told of their tasks in the family home. As little girls they helped with washing, fetching water from wells or streams in buckets made from used kerosene cans. The washing was done outdoors, sometimes in the field or under the rough shelter of porches. Having carried the water for the task, the women and girls then had to boil this in a copper, heated by a fire lit beneath the boiler. Sticks had to be collected for the fire. They might make the soap themselves from fat and soda.

Clothes were scrubbed on washing boards, blued to make the fabric white, sometimes starched before being dried on outdoor lines and then ironed with flat irons which were heated on the fire (Watson 1987: 22). Washing day was a laborious undertaking. No wonder the advent of electricity and the promise of machines to take over these tasks was warmly welcomed. Even by the 1950s a washing machine in the house was a possession to be proud of.

The photograph shows a tin bath tub like those used by families in the early years. This type of tub sometimes served a dual purpose as a receptacle in which to clean the carcase of a pig killed for the pot. Photograph by the author taken from the collection at the "Apple Museum" at Grove in the Huon Valley taken with permission 10/07/2012.

Wash day was a laborious undertaking

Wash tub or boiler with scrubbing board. Photograph by the author from the collection at the "Apple Museum" at Grove in the Huon Valley; 10/07/2012.

Clothes wringer. Photograph by the author from the collection at the "Apple Museum" at Grove in the Huon Valley; 10/07/2012.

If the woman was lucky she might wash clothes in the shelter of an outhouse or porch. If the family had the means, she might be able to wring the clothes, either in a small wringer like the one pictured above, or in a large heavy mangle like the one shown on the next page.

One tub as pictured held the soapy water for washing. The other held rinsing water. Clothes pushed through the wringer would be transferred from one tub to the other while the soapy water was directed back into the first sink. When washing was completed this water would be drained away, the rinsed clothes would be passed back through the wringer and collected in a basin or tub to be hung outside.

This photograph on the next page shows a heavy cast iron mangle. The clothes were drawn between two heavy rollers. The excess water drained down into a basin or bucket. The tension of the rollers was adjusted by turning a lever on top of the machine so that heavy articles could be fed through.

When the washing had passed through the mangle it was collected in a basket or tub and then carried outside to be hung on washing lines if the weather was fine. Wet washing might be hung to dry in the house on a "pulley", a contraption of wooden bars mounted on a frame, hung from the ceiling and raised and lowered by means of ropes.

Cast iron mangle. Photograph by the author from the collection at the "Apple Museum" at Grove in the Huon Valley; 10/07/2012.

As children, the girls scrubbed tables and floors with sandstone (Lowe 1994: 100) and painted floor surrounds with permanganate of potash crystals mixed with water, then coating them with linseed oil (Tinning 1977: 18). They made and mended their clothing and that of other family members.

If their mother was working in the orchards, the eldest girl could be left to care for younger siblings and to cook and clean for the family. With no cookery books, ingenuity was needed to make whatever was on hand into a meal for the family (Lowe 1993: 145). In two cases the girls were left in charge of the family on the early death of their mother.

Twelve of the women tell of working before marriage outside their homes on the family properties. They rounded up the cows and helped to hand milk them, they helped with feeding the pigs, collected bracken for bedding for the animals, fed the hens which were kept for eggs, packed apples, picked fruit and picked berry crops. They often were kept home from school during harvest time as their help was needed to bring in these crops. A large family to help with this task could save the farmer having to pay for outside help. This was important if the father of the family had to work hard to repay loans taken out to purchase the property.

One of the women recounts that at the age of five she was out in the berry fields looking after the younger children while the adults were picking fruit (Watson 1987: 12).

In one case, the child in question was the youngest of seven girls and then had five younger siblings. Her older sisters were all placed with neighbouring families as helpers in the homes. When another neighbour came to look for a girl to help her on her property, which she was managing alone, the nine year old volunteered to take on the task. In her autobiography, which she dictated to her son in the last years of her life, she tells of her daily routine (O'Rourke 2008).

She and her employer were up at 6am to light the fire and put on pots and a kettle. They then rounded up the cows and milked them. The milk was carried to the dairy where the older woman worked the separator while the child went to the house and prepared breakfast. She then fed the pigs and the horses before they both sat down to eat.

After breakfast she ran to school, studied during the morning and came home in the middle of the day for a meal. She returned to school before working through the evening with the cows and the rest of the stock. By nine o'clock they would have supper and she would do any homework.

On Sundays they went to Mass and had a quieter day with only the animals to attend to (O'Rourke 2008,). Nowadays not many nine year olds would not only do this work, but would profess to enjoy it.

The woman working in the dairy would separate the cream from the milk then churn the cream into butter. The butter would then be shaped using the wetted wooden butter pats which are hung on the rear wall in the display on page 23. Note the crocheted cover flung over the jug on the shelf in the photograph. With its edges weighted with beads this cover prevented flies from getting into the jug.

Some of the girls rode on horseback to collect mail and take goods to be sold. In the case of one family, (Case 2), a lack of money led to bridles being made from wattle bark and the horses were ridden bareback. It was nine miles from their home to the nearest settlement, Judbury, and further to Huonville (Fenton. In Hammond 2004: 65).

The photograph shows a reconstruction of the interior of a dairy. The milk for the day would be carried in here in pails. From the collection of the "Apple Museum" at Grove in the Huon Valley. Photograph by the author 10/07/2012.

Another lass rode her employer's horses every day after she had left school (O'Rourke 2008: 53). She rode into Cygnet on errands from the hills to the west of the township, where the land stretches down to the Huon. Yet others drove the family's horse and dray and helped care for the horse. The girls in Mrs. Tinning's family loved to take a stiff broom and sweep the stable, clearing the manure into the garden and putting chaff in the manger. They competed for the task. (Tinning 1977: 26)

Another woman recollects returning from a twelve mile drive to Huonville to collect stores to find that her brother had injured himself. She hitched the horse back to the dray, drove her injured brother from Pelverata to the Huon River and got someone to row them across through the Egg Islands canal to Franklin. She then walked her brother to the doctor at Franklin. After having the wound dressed they repeated the journey in reverse to get home She was sixteen at the time. (Lowe1993: 145).

The young women of the Huon and Channel in the early years of the century, whose stories are told in local histories, were hardy and capable in emergencies. They had to be. Sickness and injury could strike the children and did take a toll. In Case 28 the woman tells of the death of a seven year old sister whose sudden demise was such a mystery that a post-mortem was performed. In this process it was found that the child had been born with only one kidney (Watson 1987: 21). In those days there was no way this could have been known, let alone remedied.

Large family numbers were an insurance against such disasters. The woman in Case 4 relates that her mother was one of eighteen children (O'Rourke 2008: 7).

In a later interview conducted by the author in 2012, (Case 61), the woman tells of her experiences when she contracted polio as a three year old child in the late 1920s. She was taken to hospital and despite her valiant attempts to fight off the nurses, was kept there for some time before being allowed to return home. She spent the next two years confined to bed, strapped into a splint which stretched from her waist to her feet.

Even when she was eventually allowed to be free of this during the day, she continued to have to sleep with the splint in place. She was left with a life-long weakness in one of her legs. Her schooling was delayed, but when that started she walked three miles to school with the other children. A neighbour's son used to give her a lift back home, with the girl riding pillion on his bike. Mercifully, as the century progressed, immunisation has made polio, or infantile paralysis, a distant memory for parents.

Polio was still prevalent in the community when the woman in Case 63 was hospitalised with tuberculosis in the early 1940s. When she was a child she contracted TB, first in her lungs and later in her spine. She spent a period of time at Vacleuse Infectious Diseases Hospital and then Wingfield House both in Hobart. (Interview with the woman in Case 63, 2012)

Both these hospitals are mentioned in Roe (1999: 123/124). Roe (1999: 105) describes the treatment of tuberculosis in the 1930s and 1940s as being one of prescribed complete bed rest with an emphasis on a nourishing diet. Polio patients and cerebral palsy patients were also in the infectious diseases hospital and, according to the woman telling of her illness, mixed with the TB patients. At first the woman in Case 53, as a child, was in isolation in a small room of her own which looked out onto a car park. This was her only amusement, watching the cars.

When the disease appeared in her spine she underwent a bone graft.

This was just at the end of the Second World War. According to the woman, two bones from another person's spine were inserted to replace diseased vertebrae. She remembers being in a "turning bed"-- a cage like structure that fitted over her bed. The staff would place pillows on her stomach and then the contraption was inverted. She remembers the process as being very painful. She notes that while there were medical treatments there was no psychological help to deal with the trauma.

The case-studies in Roe (1999: 195) seem to confirm this assertion. Treatment was focussed upon containing the risk of further infection and of curing the patient if possible. There seems to have been little thought given to the mental effects of being removed from home and family, put into isolation, constrained to remain as motionless as possible and to endure this treatment for months. The effect of these changes being forced upon a young child, whose understanding of what was happening would have been very limited, must have been damaging to some extent at least. The woman in Case 63 remembers the trauma clearly although more than half a century has passed.

She missed a great deal of schooling and was kept relatively isolated at the home of her grandparents at Lymington near Cygnet. To compensate for missing school she had private tutorials but feels she still missed a great deal of learning. (Interview with the woman in Case 63, July 2012). She worked hard to compensate for this in later years.

A consistent theme in the stories of almost all the women was that in childhood, while there was little money, the families were always in a position to put food on the table. In the early years pigs were raised for ham and bacon. Hens provided eggs, milk from the cows provided butter and cream. Mothers baked bread and made jam from fruit. Fathers or mothers had vegetable gardens. Sometimes the diet might include eels caught in the nearby stream. One woman has described how these were nailed up by the head in order to skin them before cooking.(Interview with the woman in Case 12: April, 2012).

Rabbits flourished on the farms and were caught and eaten. One family of children set possum and wallaby traps on their way to school and collected the catch on their way home. (Lowe1993: 145).

Only one woman (Watson 1987: 21) speaks of "gracious living" and a "leisured life". Her father was an inspector at the large timber mill and also had orchard property. The family had a tennis court and boats for fishing. The children had music lessons and attended the choral society in Franklin. Shopkeepers brought their goods to the house. Then came WWI and the war changed many things, particularly the health and mental attitudes of the young men who had served there.

As the years of the twentieth century moved on, living conditions changed very little. Electricity was connected in the 1920s and 1930s to the more accessible properties in the Huon and Channel, but some households waited several more years for power to be delivered. The coming of electricity was welcome but buying appliances was costly and through the years of war and the Depression money was scarce.

Also in the 1920s the bullock cart and horse and dray began to be replaced by motor vehicles, cars in a few cases and trucks to transport crops. As motor transport became more common the roads were improved to take account of this. In turn this led to a decline in the need for transport by sea and the steamers which had plied the mouth of the Huon and the Channel were gradually made redundant, to the regret of those who had enjoyed the steamer trip to Hobart and the social occasion such a trip could be. Sitting on deck, knitting or chatting, the women would watch for friends coming aboard at the various ports of call (Tinning 1977: 29).

The girls who lost their mothers at an early age obviously had sadness in their lives. The family would grieve the loss of siblings. What is noticeable in the stories of childhood, however, is that these are described as happy years by most of the girls. As daughters, all worked hard as part of the family, but the general impression from what has been told is that these families were loving and united. Only in four cases was there a suggestion of discord within the family.

Expectations of the behaviour of children may seem strict in comparison to today's standards, corporal punishment was not unknown, but the majority of descriptions are of a warmth and enjoyment in the companionship of siblings. The women express a keen awareness that financial pressures were heavy for their parents and they accepted working for little or no reward as a natural part of their duty to the family.

Of those whose home-lives were less than happy, one of the women in the histories tells of an unhappy relationship with her father who seems to have been brutal to all his family, beating his sons and acting violently towards his first and then towards his second wife. The woman in question left home as soon as was possible and defied her father in her relationships (Watson 1987: 12 to 14).

Another tells in interview of her close friendship with family relatives, while at home there were many quarrels and difficulties and a culture of an over-dependence on alcohol in the small community. In another case, the woman tells in interview that she and her mother never got on well together, though she loved and respected her father. The fourth had decided to follow her conviction that she had a calling to enter the Church despite her father's vehement opposition.

2.2 Provision of schooling

"Our school was one room with a little cloakroom for our coats and a veranda on the front. That was a lovely little building. I was sorry when they pulled it down. I think they should have kept it as a National Trust building." (Watson 1987: 94)

In 1838 all the schools receiving Government Aid were brought under the control of a Board of Education and a code of rules and regulations were drawn up for their establishment and proper management. In the Huon however, in the early years, school accommodation was very simple and teachers were largely untrained. In 1883/84 nine buildings were discarded in favour of new property at a cost of nearly three thousand pounds. In 1879 there were nineteen schools in the Huon and Channel districts ("Centenary of the Settlement of the Huon": Huon News, 1936).

In 1903 in Glen Huon 16 children were present on the first day of school, though this number was affected by the fruit picking season. By 1917 the Glen Huon School had seventy eight students of whom fifty three are listed as Methodist, eleven as Seventh Day Adventist children (Woolley 2002). There were seven children from Mormon families and four from Anglican families. In 1921 a headmistress was in charge at Judbury School.

After the First World War an honour roll was unveiled there. The schoolteacher, a Miss Clara Lovell, had taught all but one of the men listed on the memorial (Woolley 2002: 327).

At Gordon on the Channel in 1900 there were forty one children enrolled in the school there. By 1946 the number had dropped to thirteen. A sharp drop in enrolments was attributed to the Second World War.

In 1927 a new, purpose built school had been erected at Gordon and, when the school was closed, this building was re-erected at Margate where extra classrooms were required. Kettering School had thirty six students in 1900 and in 1950 there were fifty two enrolments. This school closed in 1954.

A similar pattern existed at Middleton with fourteen children on the roll in 1900. This school was rebuilt in 1909 after a fire in 1906. In 1950 the roll was twenty nine students. The school closed around 1952 when the pupils were transferred to Woodbridge Area School (from file "Schools: Volume 1", Channel History Museum).

Outbreaks of illness could close the schools. Measles and mumps swept through the classrooms. At Glen Huon typhoid fever is reported in 1902 and 1904. The school closed during the influenza outbreak following World War 1 and diphtheria struck in 1922 and 1923.

At Glen Huon a Parents and Friends Association was formed in 1928 (Woolley 2002: 283). At Franklin the school would close if outbreaks of scarlet fever, diphtheria, measles or whooping cough struck the neighbourhood (Hayes. In Hammond 1987: 50).

In 1850 there was a public school at Lymington with an average attendance of thirty. A Mr. Lindsay became head of the public school at Port Cygnet in 1850. He was also the registrar for births, marriages and deaths in the town.

The early days at a tiny Glen Huon School building. Thirty one children are in the group. (Photograph taken from a calendar published by the Upper Huon History Group).

His salary at the school was one hundred and fifty four pounds and eight shillings per annum. According to the woman writing this history, he taught English, Spelling, Reading, Grammar, Dictation, Geography, History, Arithmetic (including Algebra and Geometry), Natural Philosophy and some French and Latin (Cockerill 1987: 3). This seems an ambitious curriculum for thirty country children. In 1886 a new school was erected.

Schools were open at Cradoc, Lymington, Wattle Grove, Glaziers Bay, Nichols Rivulet, Gardeners Bay, Deep Bay and Garden Island Creek. Excuses given for sometimes low attendance ranged from "The state of the roads in winter" to "Too many snakes" in summer (Cockerill 1987: 3).

Some of the schoolhouses (for example, at Garden Island Creek and Deep Bay) used in these years still survive as private dwellings and give a clear picture of the size and structure of the buildings the children learned in.

The Garden Island Creek schoolhouse was built in 1885 on an acre of land donated by the saw mill across the road owned by the firm Ford and Harris and leased to the Government for a peppercorn rent. It is built on a rising stand of ground which keeps the land around it dry.

The building comprised of a large classroom with two separate rooms to accommodate a teacher. One of these was a sitting room with an open fire on which meals were cooked. This fireplace is still there with the pot hooks to show where the teacher cooked her meals. (Interview with the owner of the schoolhouse, 2012).

The area on the right of the building in the first photograph on the next page is the original schoolroom, with the two rooms set aside for the teacher at the left hand side. Some of the original features remain such as the schoolroom fireplace, shown in the second photograph on the next page, and the fireplace in the teacher's sitting room. There was a cloakroom at the rear for coats.

The present owner outside the original Garden Island Creek Schoolhouse built in 1885. Photograph by the author (29/06/12)

The photograph below shows the original class room fireplace in the Garden Island Creek schoolhouse.

The Garden Island Creek schoolhouse fireplace. Photograph taken by the author with the permission of the owner in July, 2012.

In the teacher's sitting room is a similar fireplace and the hooks to hang cooking vessels are still in place. The other room was the bedroom. The teacher's accommodation was self- contained with its own front and back door. There were doors to the classroom at the front and back of the building, though the children habitually entered at the back.

School room equipment Photograph by the author from the collection at the "Apple Museum" at Grove in the Huon Valley 10/07/2012.

The photograph above shows school room equipment from the days of ink pens, slates and abacuses. The cane whose handle ominously appears in the foot left hand corner might well have been an incentive to learn the lessons and to behave in a manner pleasing to the teacher.

A list of rules for teachers is displayed in the "Apple Museum". Those for female teachers are dated 1915. Whether these rules applied in the Huon and Channel area is unclear, but certainly female teachers were not expected to marry while working under contract and would have to leave the profession, in most cases, upon marriage.

Given that Rule 6 stipulates that "You may not ride in a carriage or automobile with any man unless he is your father or brother" and Rule 2 even more firmly states "You are not to keep company with men" the chances of finding a husband under these circumstances would be difficult in the extreme. The wonder is that any women chose to enter the teaching profession.

These small schools were closed when Area schools were introduced, as at Cygnet. The Garden Island Creek School was closed in 1941. A State school had been opened in Cygnet in 1925 and in 1937 this became the first Area school in Southern Tasmania with a

Mr. Benjamin appointed as head teacher. Children were brought there by bus from all the small schools and the roll rose to three hundred and seventy pupils. The subjects taught then ranged from the basics of sewing and cooking, woodwork, black-smithing, tin-smithing, the care of fowls, growing vegetables and fruit, to picking and pruning apples (Cockerill 1987: 4).

This practical curriculum varies greatly from that claimed for the Port Cygnet School in 1850. The change could not be said to lead to more academic aspirations for the students, but given the period immediately following the Depression such skills must have been thought more useful. "The children cooked three course meals which were served to the bus children." (Cockerill 1987: 4) In later years the school at Cygnet reverted to a primary school.

For those children brought up in the Catholic faith a school was opened in Cygnet by the Sisters of St. Joseph. This school was the successor to a Roman Catholic Church School run by a Mrs. Phillips in 1878. The Sisters of St. Joseph taught the children at St. Mary's, as it was then (Cockerill 1987: 4).

The buildings which housed this school are still in use, with the school room now used as a café/restaurant. Later these buildings were enlarged to become the St. James Parish School and the Sisters ran this until 1972.

The woman in Case 69 attended this school in the 1950s and 1960s and recollects, with much fondness, the kindness and encouragement of the young nuns who were her teachers. The woman notes that as she went through school it became more common for lay-women to take over the teaching duties in the classrooms. The number of religious vocations dwindled and, while the convent buildings still stand in Cygnet, an interview in 2012 showed that now only a few elderly Sisters still live there.

2.3 Education for the girls.

"I liked school. I always enjoyed it. I think it's a very happy time of your life—you haven't got any worries. We didn't get half the things kiddies get now, but we didn't look for it. We were happy." (Watson 1987: 95)

Two of the women in the study were educated at home by

governesses (Lowe 199: 27. Tinning 1977: 24). The others were likely to be educated at local schools. In the earlier years of the century fourteen of the women mention schooling in the telling of their stories, but only seven specify the name of their school. One started her schooling at Wattle Grove soon after that school opened on a full time basis. Before that date, her older sister walked six kilometres to school at the convent of the Sisters of St. Joseph, in Cygnet (O'Rourke 2008: 5).

The school at Wattle Grove had been opened under the control of the Education Department of Tasmania in 1874. At first, because of the sparse population of the district the school was open on a half-time basis only, but requests from the residents saw it opened full-time in 1898 (a few years before the woman in Case 4 would have been old enough to attend).

The teacher appointed was a Miss Marion Oldham, a native of Hobart who had taught in the town before being posted to Wattle Grove (O'Rourke 2008: 9). The roll of the school was, on average, 24 pupils with a record attendance of 28.

The school this same woman next attended (Case 4) was at Glazier's Bay. That school was erected in in June 1898. The building was situated about one and a half miles from the bay. Port Cygnet was three and a half miles away. The school itself consisted of one room measuring 18 feet by 23 feet and in 1900 the roll was 25 students. The first teacher there was Mr. Reuben Judd.

Subsequently, Mr. Judd must have been replaced by a female teacher because the woman in Case 4 speaks with great admiration of her. She arrived late in the woman's time at school. This teacher had come from Queensland and had been a governess in Cygnet before taking up the post. She introduced her students to readings from Shakespeare and to a much wider curriculum than they had been accustomed to receive. Sadly this young teacher was married to "an uncouth fellow" and was a victim of his violence. The marriage failed and she moved to Hobart. (O'Rourke 2008: 45)

As with the lass who walked six kilometres to reach school, many of the girls faced a long walk each day. This walk was readily accepted as the norm. In fact, the exercise was considered a benefit to the girls. It must be remembered that walking long distances would be a normal part of everyday existence for most of the residents of the Huon and Channel. At one stage in the not-so-distant past the mailman would walk from Hobart to the Huon Valley over the mountain tracks (Hammond. In Hammond 2004: 17).

In the early years, with the girls having spent around seven years in schooling, family circumstances and a lack of money, added to by the absence of any further provision for schooling in the area, precluded most of the children taking the opportunity to progress to further years of education. Intelligence or diligence made no difference to the outcomes because of a lack of family funds and the remoteness of their homes.

In Case 50, the woman telling her story provides a vivid description of her school in Tiers Road at Snug. She comments that schools in rural areas were very primitive by modern standards and had very little by way of equipment. Her school in Tiers Road had one room which housed as many as six classes. Each class had a designated row in the room and a huge fire warmed the space. The teachers were Mr. Portnell, Miss Daft and Mr. Beresford. The teachers worked from a high desk at the front of the room. There were four school terms in the year with a week's holiday between, except at Christmas when four weeks holiday was allowed. This coincided with the berry picking season (Lowe undated: 26).

In Case 57, the woman attended Glazier's Bay School. The school had one big room with a fireplace. There was one long desk while she was there. The teacher avoided wearing white trousers in case ink was splattered on them. The children worked with slates and chalk, then lead pencils and finally pens with ink in inkwells (Cygnet Living History Museum, Oral History Folder 10) The basic services provided by small local schools of under a hundred pupils meant that the pupils would learn to read and write and to work out simple arithmetical problems.

A teacher with thirty to fifty students, with ages varying from six or seven to fourteen, and working alone could not be expected to offer more. An annual event might be the arrival of education inspectors, something of an ordeal for staff and pupils alike. (Lowe undated: 26) Yet, like the woman in Case 4 and, much later, the woman in Case 69, many of the girls may have welcomed a glimpse of the world outside their valley and coastal districts, which a gifted teacher would provide.

Fifty eight of the women in the earlier years of the study seem to have received at least a rudimentary education. The exception was the woman in Case 52 who, having been denied an education, could neither read nor write (Lowe undated: 36/37). Parents may have had very little education themselves and may have seen little need for their children to access more. They seem to have been quite content to withdraw their sons and daughters from the schools if family needs demanded this.

One young man, withdrawn from school at eleven to work in the orchards, is later to complain about his lack of education. His aunt is reported to have replied. "What are you complaining about? You can read and write, can't you?" (O'Rourke 2008: 49)

Harvest time stretched from February onwards till the crops were brought in. The girls worked alongside their families and if the harvest coincided with the school term, then school was missed. At Glen Huon School in 1925, only one little girl starting school for the first time was in class on the opening day of the school year (Woolley 2002: 279).

The berry crops were first to be picked. The work would last all day from early morning till about 5pm. A set target was expected from each picker and even the children had to achieve this. For some families the picking season meant moving from home to stay in "pickers' huts" on neighbouring properties. Despite the hard work, this break in routine was regarded as something of a holiday (Lowe 1994: 29).

The wages paid were welcome as a source of income earned by the mother and her children to supplement the father's wages or to support him in his payments for his land. If the family was large then the children would form the backbone of the harvest workforce (Watson 1987: 52).

The school at Glazier's Bay had one big room with a fireplace. At the time the woman in Case 4 attended there was one long desk. (Cygnet Living History Museum Oral History Folder 10. C.L.H.-00227)

An account to me from an elderly, local farmer tells that two of his aunts were teachers at Deep Bay and Gardeners Bay respectively. There was no school house at Deep Bay at the time so the sisters lived together at the Gardeners Bay schoolhouse and one took her pony and trap down to Deep Bay each morning. The pony was left on their father's farm and he hitched it back to the trap at the end of the school day for the return home.

"Country Schools were very primitive by today's standards and very little was available by way of equipment." (Lowe undated: 28)

In the latter years of this study from the mid-twentieth century onward, opportunities for young women became slightly wider. School buses transported the girls to area schools. School classes now existed for Years 7, 8, 9 and 10. One woman (Case 69) describes her Grade 1 classroom. The room was "beautifully decorated" with a mural showing coloured fish as if they were swimming in an aquarium. Alongside this was an alphabet section from which they learned their letters. Although her time in the infant class would have been in the 1950s, slates and chalk were still in use to practice writing but the ethos of the classroom seems much like many in the present day.

She also tells of being taught by a young woman who had worked on the West Coast of Tasmania and included geology in her science curriculum. In addition this teacher introduced her pupils to chemistry, astronomy, ancient architecture, poetry and English literature. Sewing and home economics were still a large component in the curriculum for girls, but horizons were widening.

In 1937 New Town Commercial High School opened in the northern suburbs of Hobart. In 1940 the school was renamed Ogilvie after a past Premier of the State. Three of the women travelled to

Hobart to further their education in secretarial studies. Because daily travel to Hobart was still difficult this meant boarding in the town. Later daily bus services allowed at least one of them to remain at home and commute to her studies.

2.4 Adolescent years between school and marriage

> *"When I left school I was picking as well as doing the housework. I'd carry the cases out for Dad. Dad would cart all day for……..then he'd come home and cart what I had picked, then my sister and I would stand and grade them—you put them through rings—and Dad would pack them. It was only small but we managed with Dad working really hard." (Watson 1987: 43)*

The majority of the women whose lives are recorded in local histories were the daughters of farmers or orchardists. The stories of their lives are filled with details of life on the land. The men-folk sometimes combined farming with timber cutting, for example to make boxes for the apple crop.

The soil was found to be suitable for the production of fruit, apples and pears and for berry fruits. The orchard industry was established. By 1840 apples were being shipped abroad. In 1884 a first trial shipment went to London. By 1914 a million cases were shipped. By 1926 the total had risen to three million. By 1936 apple and pear orchards stretched almost continuously from Huonville to Cygnet (Hammond. In Hammond 1987:16). Owning orchards was a precarious way of making a living. The crop could be damaged by weather. Markets might fail. Shipping might not be available.

For the majority of the girls, leaving school meant moving into the family workforce. In the case of the woman quoted above, who had taken over the role of housewife at the age of fourteen on the death of her mother, she not only did the housework but picked apples and would stand with her sister in the evenings and grade apples while her father packed (Watson 1987: 43).

Another describes working only for her keep and seven pounds at the end of the season, because her father was fully committed to buying the property (Watson 1987: 95). She and her mother and sister packed about 11,000 cases. Each box might contain 300 apples each of which had to be wrapped in paper. The family worked from 7.30am till late at night with time off only for meals.

There is an anecdote in one of the stories which seems to encapsulate the spirit of harvest days. One of the women, who came to help the family pick, always celebrated her birthday during the raspberry season and "her present was always a cowpat wrapped in newspaper." This joke repeated through the years and always provided merriment for the recipient as well as for those around her (Lowe 1993: 29).

The woman who told this story lives (at the time she was interviewed) on the same property that was owned by her mother and father. The apple shed in which they worked still stands at the back of the home, though the orchards are long gone and thirty five dwellings now occupy that space (conversation with Madge Lowe April 2012).

In the words of another woman, there was a lot of work to be done and everyone had to help. She was one of a large family and because of this her father did not require to pay pickers to come in. (Watson 1987: 52)

Fifteen of the women whose stories are told in local histories worked outside the family property. One went at thirteen to work in the local butcher's shop for three shillings a week (Lowe, 1994: 97). Another, whose case has already been discussed, was nine when she left home to work for a neighbour (O'Rourke 2008: 37). Yet another took up a post as a nanny in Sandy Bay before her marriage (Lowe 1993: 133). Caring for other people's children was also a role undertaken by the woman in Case 13 (Lowe 1994: 32). Another of the women left home for a brief period to work in the nearby township. She was very homesick and soon returned to help her mother (Watson 1987: 55).

The woman whose father was brutal to his family left home as soon as possible to work as a housekeeper on a neighbouring property, having for a brief spell worked in Hobart (Watson 1987: 13).

Nine of the women in total worked in Hobart after finishing school. For at least two this meant boarding in the city and coming home at weekends (Lowe 1993: 31). One of these (Case 53) went from Kettering State School to Remington Business College in Hobart and then worked for Gestetner and in the public service (Lowe undated: 45). Another worked in an office in Hobart before spending some time in Sydney, then returning to Tasmania (Case 12).

Most of these women were among the younger people in the group identified by local historians, so their journeys were facilitated by buses being available. At this time young women, for example Case 12, could become involved in social activities such as Cub Scouts, playing organ in the church and forming dance bands.

One sad case reported is that of the woman who was sent to Hobart to work as a maid in exchange for receiving an education. Her workload increased but the promised education was not provided, leaving her functionally illiterate (Lowe undated: 36). In Case 38, the woman interviewed began teaching in Longley and then at Triabunna before returning to Sandfly (Lowe undated: 53). As the century progressed into the 1950s and 1960s and to the latter years, data from interviews has shown that more women in the area were moving into the workforce outside the family farm. For two (Cases 69 and 73) this meant employment in local offices or shops. For two others teaching careers were entered into.

Working in local shops was a respectable occupation for young women which allowed them to remain near to their homes.

Chapter 3: Home grown entertainment

3.1 The early years

"While the entertainments may not have been sophisticated, they were an authentic expression of the interests of the residents. As communication with Hobart was difficult, particularly in the evening, entertainment had to be locally based. This "enforced" social interaction served to build a strong sense of community identity and mutual responsibility and caring...." (Gardam 1992: 44)

Another aspect of the period between school and marriage for the women has been the social life of the communities. What is clear from research into the early years of the study is that a sense of community and social cohesion was a source of strength to the women in the study.

In the introduction to "Full and Plenty" (Watson 1987), it is noted that many of the women in the Huon in the first half of the twentieth century lived their lives in and around the district in which they were born, sometimes in the same house that had been the family home for generations. Travelling to Hobart was a rare outing. A trip by steamer to Hobart meant a day's journey, not to be undertaken frequently. To reach the nearest centre, Huonville, from Pelverata, was a twelve mile trip by horse and dray (Lowe 1994: 97).

Travelling to the mainland or abroad was almost unheard of. Only one woman went to live abroad (Redeker. In Hammond 2004: 22). Another was offered the opportunity to accompany her employers overseas but rejected this and returned to the Huon (Watson 1987: 14). In one memoir the woman came to live in the Channel from England and left the area later to move elsewhere in Tasmania (Tinning 1977: 48).

For young men the case may have been different. The period under discussion saw the First World War in Europe and the Middle East, followed by the Second World War. One reason given by the women for their brothers' enlistment was that this would be a chance for travel and adventure (Watson 1987: 21). Sadly, for many, the adventure cost their lives.

In the earliest years the condition of roads and a lack of transport meant that entertainment was mostly based within the home or the homes of near neighbours. Families and friends might gather around the piano to listen to music or to join in singing. Card games might feature as a part of the occasion (Gardam 2007: 119). Stories would be exchanged and local gossip might circulate.

3.2 Later in the century

As the years passed, and with the advent of motorised vehicles, roads were improved. Community halls became local centres. Dances formed a major part of the expanding social scene. At Snug, for instance, according to Gardam (2007), as well as dances, the community enjoyed concerts and lantern shows. Not only were these events well patronised but they raised funds for local causes.

In many homes a piano or harmonium held pride of place. These instruments were the focus of entertainment and sometimes church services. Photograph by the author with permission from the collection at the "Apple Museum" at Grove in the Huon Valley 10/07/2012.

Families would gather round the piano to listen and to sing.

The dances proved to be a welcome opportunity for the young women to dress in their best. These dresses were sewed at home by lantern light (Lowe 1994: 97). After hard work around the house or on the property the girls had a chance to shine in local society. To be sure, this opportunity might come after a long walk to reach the venue, or a journey by boat across the Huon, a bumpy ride in a horse and cart or, later, a bicycle ride with dresses tucked up to avoid the pedals and chain.

Permission to attend in the first place had to be sought from parents and if, as in one case, fathers disapproved of make-up then this had to be carried to the hall, then applied. At the end of the dance, like Cinderella, all traces of the make-up must be removed before returning home (Lowe 1994: 97).

One outcome of the dance might be the introduction of a young woman to a young man "and we were married within twelve months." (Watson 1987: 6) Sophisticated the entertainment might not be, with music provided by "Bert Gallacher's dad on the melodeon" (Gardam 1997: 43), but the simplicity suited the lifestyle of the communities. Later, dance bands were formed such as the Cygnet Joyspreaders and the Middleton Melody Makers. As this level of sophistication crept in, the halls would host Mr. Perry's Travelling Talkies.

The movie nights were fitted in between regular dance nights. One mother drove her boys to the movies and treated them to Violet Crumble bars (Lowe 1994: 126). In another family, an uncle would drive the children to Kermandie to see the show, wait for them in the pub and then drive them home. This was a rare treat (Watson 1987: 43). The "Travelling Talkies" continued for nearly half a century, ending with Dick Perry's retirement in 1972 ("People of the Channel": File from the Channel Heritage Museum).

An exception to the generally male dominated sports scene was in Sandfly where a teacher who was a keen hockey player formed the girls into a competitive team. Much later in the century there are descriptions of women taking up the game of golf and of playing netball.

Another opportunity to dress in finery may have been a debutante ball, held to mark a young woman's entry into local society. These, again, had been modelled on the London practice of presentation to the King and Queen at Buckingham palace of young women from the upper echelons of British society. These local events were formal, with the girls partnered by their escorts in choreographed dance and a presentation to a local dignitary complete with curtsey.

Boats on the river could be transport to a dance. Photograph from the collection of Steve Lucas

Chapter 4: Life following marriage

4.1 Marriage

"Her story is that of many pioneering women who made Australia. They were stoics, who lived unselfish isolated lives, striving to provide comfort for their families with minimal facilities. These women are our history's unsung heroes." (Fenton. In Hammond 2004: 66)

Marriage was the norm for the women. Of the seventy five women in this study, only five women identify themselves as not having married. "No one asked me and in any case I didn't have time." (Hayes. In Hammond 2004: 50). One of the five entered a religious order (Case 61). Three of the fifty nine women in Part 1 were unmarried.

From the recollections of the women, there would appear to have been a degree of simplicity in the marriage ceremonies in the early years of the century which fitted economic and social conditions. Marriages were family affairs with a reception in the local hall, or perhaps a cup of tea at a relative's house (Lowe undated: 133).

In at least one case, the bride and groom eloped to Hobart, travelling there by bus and without having to pay their fare when the bus driver learned of the purpose of the trip (Lowe 1994: 49). Revenge for a father's domineering behaviour brought about another marriage "I married to beat my father." (Watson 1987: 14).

The women living through wars and Depression had known from early childhood that money was usually scarce Most of them knew that their families struggled to make ends meet. The sort of lavish white wedding common in present times would have been far out of reach for many. Nor was a honeymoon part of the plan. One woman states, in a matter-of-fact manner, that she got married one day and was out picking berry fruit the next (Watson 1987: 14).

These details of simple weddings contrast with a later events. Post War prosperity had obviously allowed far more lavish occasions to be planned. Four of the girls in the study were married while they were still teenagers (Cases 15, 26, 27, 71). Twenty four of the women married farmers or orchardists. In the case of these women, apart from pregnancies and raising a family, their lives would have continued in much the same way as they had done throughout their single years. For three of the women the care of older relatives was part of their duties as well as the housework and child rearing. (Cases 6, 13, 36)

Not all the women in the earlier years were fully occupied at home or on a property. As with all small communities there were a variety of roles which needed to be filled. Three helped their husbands in working in local Post Offices or shops (Cases 9, 17, 50). One woman ran a shop with her daughter (Case 33). One woman known as Gypsy Peg made and sold clothes pegs and travelled the whole district in her horse and cart, sleeping beside her children and dogs under the cart (Gardam 2007: 132).

One woman, who did not marry, worked as a shop assistant in Hobart (Case 37). Yet another woman worked as a civilian at the Barracks in Hobart during the Second World War.(Case 40).

Another was a schoolteacher for twenty nine years (Case 38). The woman in Case29, who never married , took over the running of her uncle's orchards and made a career as an orchardist. She became a respected authority, holding leadership positions and speaking in public and acting as a lay preacher in the Uniting Church for many years. Her widowed sister who had six children moved in to live with her. Little wonder she had no time to marry. She lived (and still lives at the time of writing) a very full, independent life.

In the later years of the century women with whom I have spoken still followed well-trodden career paths, in office work and management, in serving in shops, in teaching, in working with children. Three of these women spoke about ambitions they might have had to try careers to which they were more attracted. One spoke of wanting to join the police or the army, but had her ideas ridiculed by her family. One described her ambition to work in a plant nursery, while in reality she was directed into office work. The third had watched her grandmother work as a tailor and loved fabric and craft work. Her mother insisted she get office training and she made a successful career in this field before being able in retirement to concentrate on her initial enthusiasm for crafts.

They came to small homes surrounded by gardens and orchards

Bridal finery from the earlier years of the 20th.Century. Photograph from the collection of Steve Lucas.

Bride in the 1950s. Photograph used with the permission of Madge Lowe.

1960s wedding at Middleton. Photograph from the collection of the South Channel Progress Association.

In "Playing Our part" (CWA 1996), it is noted that the norm around 1936 was that women were known after marriage by their husband's name, for example Mrs. William Smith. This designation would be used in public on formal occasions and would have fitted with the convention of wearing hats and gloves on such occasions (CWA 1996). Married women would no longer be part of the paid work force.

This study shows, however, that the labour of married women and their children on the farms and orchards of the Huon and Channel was very much a part of community expectations. These formal conventions and expectations have largely disappeared by the latter years of the twentieth century. Two of the women who shared their stories with me have never taken their husband's surname, preferring to use their birth surname. This would have been unthinkable in earlier years.

4.2 Motherhood

Most women in the early years took it for granted that they would marry and raise families. On the untimely death of a husband they would work to raise that family or would remarry (Lowe undated: 37 : Watson 1987: 55). In the absence of educational skills and the lack of career paths, re-marriage would be a sensible course.

One woman in the early years had ten children by her first husband. On his death she re-married a widower, also with ten children and they raised a combined family of twenty. Not only were large families seen as natural, but infant mortality and sickness might be expected to take a toll on young children. Large family numbers were an insurance against such disasters. One woman lost two brothers to TB (Watson 1987: 52) and another lost her brother to a heart condition following service in World War I (Watson 1987: 21).

Health services were basic and the dangers to health, obvious in the present enlightened times, were probably little understood then. Water was brought from streams and wells, wells that at times might be contaminated by faecal matter (O'Rourke 2008: 82). Typhus and cholera occurred. Sanitation was primitive. One woman awarded the invention of the septic tank the top prize for life- changing innovations (interview with woman in Case 12, 2012). Tuberculosis was an ever present threat and the infectious nature of this killer was not properly understood. After World War I, the seemingly innocuous influenza carried away many victims. More ordinary, but sometimes life threatening, were the normal childhood illnesses of measles, whooping cough, chicken pox and mumps. Outbreaks of these could cause schools to close.

Often a mother was the source of nursing for her family and a list of home cures appears on page 51. Others had more training or general experience and could be called in when home nursing would not be enough. .One woman was the local midwife in addition to her family role (Case 8). Another started a home nursing service in the Channel, driving herself around the townships (Gardam 2007: 137).

One woman (Case 39) opened a small hospital in Judbury, an area where medical help was hard to reach (Lowe undated: 55). In Cygnet, according to Cockerill (1987), by around 1900 a Matron Adams worked with Dr. Wade and ran a small hospital in Louisa Street. A Bush Nursing Service had been founded and the help of these nurses saved lives. In one case the woman recalls that the nearest doctor was five miles away and had to be sent for, then would come by horse and cart (Watson 1987).

Help would be a long time in reaching the patient (Watson 1987: 21). Another woman comments that the family didn't use the doctor in Franklin much because you had to travel so far (Watson 1987: 7). A family in Birches Bay (Case 16) note that the nearest doctor was in Snug, so home remedies were all they had (Lowe 1994: 126). This was during the 1940s. At one stage the population of Gordon had to send to Cygnet if a doctor was required. Gardam (undated: 90) tells of an old lady being taken from her sick bed by her well-meaning carers to be made to stand knee deep in the sea—because the doctor's instructions stated that her medicine "should be taken in water"!

Because doctors were few and far between, midwifes attended many births. They were local women with experience in delivering babies. One such was Mrs. Phillips, over on the Channel in the early years (Gardam undated: 90). In the Geeveston district one of the daughters of the Geeves family, Mrs. Whewell, was the local midwife at this early stage of development. There were no maternity hospitals even in Hobart. Mrs. Roberts was the midwife at Cygnet. Mrs. Talbot was midwife at Huonville and Mrs. Phillips at Three Hut Point (Gardam undated: 90: Garnsey 1944). Some women travelled to Hobart to give birth in the relative safety of a larger town, a journey not to be undertaken lightly given travel conditions. (O'Rourke 2008: 9) This choice was not always open to them. As late in the century as the decade of the 1960s, the woman in Case 64 concedes that, despite her mother's somewhat cold nature she was an excellent nurse and cared for many of those around her. This same mother had had very little education so her skills were inborn rather than taught.

Table 1: List of home cures (taken from Lowe, 1993, O'Malley, 2009 and interview data)

Problem	Cure
Infected eye	Rub wedding ring around eyes to cure infected area.
Throat infections	Kerosene and sugar for a sore throat
Coughs and colds	Irish Moss for colds
Toothache	Oil of Cloves+ a hot water bottle if necessary to cure toothache
Protection	Pinned camphor bags to the children's vests to ward off germs
Backache/chills	Red flannel belt worn for backache and chills
Infected sores	Bread poultices
For infected fingers	Break a hole in an egg and stick infected finger into the yolk
Hair restorers	Use Brandy + salt to restore hair—or sheep dip
Hangovers	Worcestershire sauce
General illness	Castor oil was a universal remedy
Stomach upsets	Milk of Magnesia
Worm infestation	A mixture of Sulphur and treacle
Protection from colds	Cod liver oil, Vicks Vapour Rub
Cure almost anything	Paraffin oil
General health	Home- made rose-hip syrup
Severe Headache	Soak brown paper bag in vinegar and apply to skull
Pregnancy	Suspend wedding ring over abdomen. The direction in which the ring rotates indicates the sex of the child

The biographies of the women researched in the course of this study provide two harrowing stories in the course of childbirth in the early days of the twentieth century. Childbirth was dangerous.

The woman in Case 4, herself the seventh daughter in the family, tells of her mother's delivery of twins. Her mother was left alone in their house when labour had started as her husband and daughter had left to get assistance. The younger children were sent to a neighbouring house. While everyone was gone the twins made their entry to the world. The little boy had a caul covering his head which his mother was able to break through. She then lost consciousness . When help arrived and the babies were seen to be healthy, they then revived her. (O'Rourke 2008: 9)

This same mother gave birth to her tenth child prematurely. After the birth she was very ill and underwent an operation in Hobart to remove a large benign tumour. She was away from home in Hobart for a long time. She never really got over this major operation (O'Rourke 2008: 17).

In Case 27, the woman tells of having the doctor present at her first two deliveries. The deliveries were difficult but there was nothing given to help. The doctor charged six guineas for his services. With her last four children she managed without him. She notes that she (and probably many others) had little knowledge of the "facts of life". Sex education was certainly not a topic on the school curriculum. She was married at eighteen. The woman asked a female relative for advice during pregnancy but then felt foolish and wished she had not (Watson 1987: 17).

Occasionally, desperation would mean a woman sought an end to a pregnancy. One horrible case that illustrates such desperation is vividly documented anecdotally. A woman with six small children attempted to abort her seventh pregnancy. When she was found she was near to death. Her children were huddled in a corner, terrified. Neighbours took the children and cared for them, but the woman could not be saved. (Watson 1987: 22)

In another case a woman dying of cancer makes arrangements for her large family to be taken in and cared for by the Catholic Church. She cannot leave them alone and knows that her husband would be unable to care for them. (O'Rourke 2008: 32)

The former Bowmont Hospital building in Franklin still fronts the main road though in 2013 it is used as an antiques saleroom. In the mid-years of the twentieth century it functioned as a maternity hospital. The women in Case 65 and case 71 were born in the building. There was a six bed maternity unit. The woman in Case 60 worked there as a nurse's assistant and shared a room on the upper floor with a colleague. The nurses' home was then moved to a property nearby and the upstairs was converted to general wards. At this time the decorative knobs on the stairway banisters had to be removed as, in the event of patient death, the knobs prevented a coffin being negotiated down the stairs. (Interview with the woman in Case 60)

When mothers died early the eldest daughter was often given the task of raising younger siblings. The woman in Case 30 was twelve when she left school to run her home. She was fortunate to have the help and advice of her grandmother and aunt (Watson 1987: 42).

The outcomes for women becoming pregnant outside marriage were even more dire. This would have been true in most societies at that time. Many may have married in haste. In some families the newborn may simply have been absorbed into the rest of the family brood as part of its grandmother's family (McCalman 1993: 130). In Case 4, the woman comments on local disapproval of an unmarried mother who raised her child. She also noted that the young woman made a good and responsible mother (O'Rourke 2008: 63). Others, in her situation, chose to risk abortion though this was an illegal act. In the middle years of the twentieth century, women still faced these harsh choices. One is said to have married the father of her unborn child, ignoring her parents' wishes. Her father cut off all contact with her family so that his grandchildren never officially met him. One of these grandchildren who, in late childhood, talked to him and introduced herself met with no acknowledgement. (Case 69: Interview 2013)

In another case in the same community a woman was refused permission to marry and this time conformed to her mother's wishes. She raised her child as a single parent but they were isolated and mocked by others in the community (Interview 2013).

For women who conceived a child out of wedlock, publicity over recent years has highlighted a practice of removing babies for adoption without the full consent of the mother. In the twenty first century women are coming forward to testify that, as late as the 1960s, they were drugged heavily during the birth process, were never given an opportunity to see their child and were refused any information as to what had become of the baby. Social norms at the time encouraged this course of action.

By the 1930s there was a small maternity hospital in Cygnet with room for eight patients. This is described by the woman in Case 59 (Cygnet Living History Museum, Folder 1) .

There were incidences reported of domestic violence. Only four of those instances directly affected the women in the study, one of whose father "was very strict" (Watson 1987: 12). Her mother left home when the woman was four, perhaps because of his violence. His second wife accepted that he would hit her. He would force his sons to strip naked before beating them. He beat the woman in the study with a stick to force her to give up a relationship he disapproved of. She defied him. (Case 27) The woman in Case 4 tells of witnessing a husband beating his teacher wife, while the students, hearing screams, watched helplessly (O'Rourke 2008: 45). The woman in Case 18 was whipped as a child for picking a neighbour's flowers (Lowe 1994: 97). In Case 69 the woman tells of her mother acting violently towards her. In Case 69 the difficulties the family faced were caused by an over-consumption of alcohol in the home. This, in addition to the ill-health of the father caused displays of temper and threats of harm. For the woman telling of these events the help of kinsfolk and friends protected her.

In Case 4 the plight of a poor family with a brutal father is described. The woman telling the story points out that there was no help available, apart from whatever the neighbours might provide.

Fortunately, as she comments, neighbours were usually very generous (O'Rourke 2008: 24).

To balance these reports of brutality, there are acknowledgements of the hard work fathers carried out to clear their land and expressions of admiration for this toil. In a tribute to her father the woman in Case 42 writes that her father was kindly, just and courteous, capable of dealing with whatever life brought to him and her ideal, who never let her down (Tinning 1977: 32). In the evenings she and her mother and sisters would sit and mend or sew clothing while he read to them from classical stories.

The women in the study accepted that their husbands worked long hours and in difficult circumstances. Managing a farm or an orchard left the family open to natural disasters, to events from the outside world which were beyond their control, to disappointment and sometimes to the loss of the property which they had worked so hard to clear and to care for. For the male breadwinner in the Channel the opening of the Carbide works at Electrona provided an additional source of income, but one which meant fitting caring for their property around working factory shifts. The history of the works, however, indicates that its future was often in doubt, with closures and changes of ownership (Townsley 1991: 290).

For the women, work in their homes in the earlier years of the twentieth century was as time-consuming and difficult as it had been in their childhood and was made more so by rearing and having to care for their children. For at least one woman (Case 2) even in the 1930s, having followed her husband to a remote bush property nine miles beyond Judbury, life was basic in the extreme. Her husband spent a great deal of time doing what he loved best, being out in the bush prospecting or timber clearing. She was left alone to raise four children, run the property and to live in a bush hut similar to that described in the earliest days of settlement. Her daughters slept in a tent in the garden. Her son's bed was a couch in the living area. To this far-flung house site she somehow had a piano and harmonium transported from her parent's home. She planted and grew flowers as well as vegetables. She provided her children with the basics of education. The family was so poor that the children often went barefoot. Her health suffered.

In a final irony, she had gone for rest to her brother's home when a bushfire struck in 1934. Her son, who had been left in charge of the property, managed to load her piano onto the bullock dray and drag it to safety, but he could do nothing to save their home. The woman died shortly after this fire (Fenton. In Hammond 2004: 66).

In a much later case in the 1950s, the early death of her husband meant that the woman, with two small daughters, took over the running of the farm and orchard. She learned to drive at this time as a necessity. In the 1967 bushfires she defended the property single-handedly until forced to evacuate (Case 71: Interview 2013).

At Hartzview Winery, in the hills above Nichols Rivulet, the proprietors have reconstructed the pickers' huts on the property and have had the village listed as a heritage site. The interiors of the cottages have been furnished to give some idea of living conditions and this reconstruction may illustrate the living conditions described in some of the women's stories.

Fireplace in one of the pickers huts. Photograph taken with permission from the owners of Hartzview vineyard.

The bare essentials of furniture were present, a great deal of it hand made to save money. One woman dipped hessian in cochineal to make curtains for the windows of what was described as little more than a "pickers' hut" down near the water at Snug (Lowe 1994: 49). Some of the floors were of beaten earth, while others had wooden boards. She covered the earth with hessian bags. This again was in the 1930s. The family had moved there to be near to the husband's work at Electrona.

After years of work on a second family home in Snug to make this comfortable, bushfires struck in 1967 and everything was destroyed (Lowe 1993: 49).

The interior of the restored pickers' huts at Hartzview Winery in the hills between Woodbridge and Nichols Rivulet. (By permission of the owners of the vineyard)

Another interior of the restored pickers' huts at Hartzview Winery. (By permission of the owners of the vineyard)

4.3 Community support

"Everyone knew everyone else and you never locked your door. We had a big old fireplace and we'd have logs at the back door. It would be nothing in those days to get up in the morning and find someone lying inside in front of the fireplace. People would go around looking for work and they would walk in and lie down. Then you would give them their breakfast and they'd be on their way. You always opened your home, you never closed your home up......so you could help wanderers on their way." (Cygnet Living History Museum Oral Folder 10, C.L.H.-00227)

Another consistent theme in the research is the sense of community and the help extended by neighbours if things went wrong. Nearly all the women remained in their communities. A woman managing her property alone apart from the help of the nine year old girl could look for assistance or advice from male neighbours in tasks that were beyond her (O'Rourke 2008, P.59). If bereavement occurred the neighbours would show their respect by drawing down house blinds and assisting with the funeral. One woman was known for offering more practical help by expressing her sorrow and then taking away washing which had to be done to relieve the mourning family (Watson 1987: 22). In the case of the poor mother who lost her life to abortion, neighbouring families took over the care of her six children. A woman working after the death of her husband in a work-related accident found that if she was walking home late in the day a neighbour would come to meet her (Watson 1987: 55).

The closeness of the communities and the remoteness from outside help in the early years of the century explains this self-supporting relationship. It has been said that everyone knew everyone else and in some cases would have known their parents and grandparents. Close bonds were forged in blood kinship and in friendship. Perhaps feuds erupted but, if this was so, the women telling their family histories seldom disclosed these facts. What is apparent is that help offered was welcomed and would be reciprocated when the need arose.

The role of Churches was undoubtedly strong in the communities. The services of priests and ministers would be needed for marriages, baptisms and funerals. On Sundays, however, cows still had to be milked, animals fed and food prepared. The life of a family on the land might make church attendance mandatory, but something to be fitted in to more vital concerns. Several of the women telling of their lives note an involvement in their local church, as lay preacher, organist or a secretary for church business. One (Case 61), interviewed by the author, decided as a young woman that she would join a religious order and did so despite her father's reservations. Another was involved in liturgical work as part of her teaching duties (Case 63). Others volunteered for roles in youth organisations such as Guides and Cubs. The Red Cross organised voluntary work during the two World Wars. By the 1930s the Countrywomen's Association had been formed and was providing an outlet for community service, as well as a forum for public speaking and a chance to demonstrate household skills in baking, jam-making and cooking. Another woman who was interviewed was local president of a CWA branch (Case 62).

4.4 Women's suffrage

In the early years of the twentieth century the right to vote was gradually extended to women. By 1911 it was compulsory to enrol to vote. Despite this catalogue of increased opportunities and responsibilities for women, while Alexander (1991) notes that by 1914 women were joining women's organizations throughout the State, no mention of political involvement appears in the case-studies identified in the early part of the twentieth century. Though careers were increasingly seen as an alternative to marriage, there was however, according to Alexander, no organized pressure for women's rights. No strong feminist leader emerged, there was no women's press and no challenge by working class women. Middle class women wanted self-determination in practical rather than abstract terms (Alexander 1991).

Data from the early years of the present study supports the findings of Alexander. In the sixty case studies identified in the early years of the twentieth century there is absolutely no mention of women's suffrage as playing a significant role in the lives of the women. There is no evidence of political allegiances, no mention of voting rights and, apart from one footnote that a husband served as a local councillor (Case 14), no interest shown in politics at all.

Again it has to be remembered that the case-study data which deals with the early years of the century is taken from the work of local historians. The preponderant data in these works is focussed on the lives of men in the communities.

It is possible that questions regarding politics were skewed towards these men. Since there is no record of the questions asked of either men or women, this is difficult to ascertain. The absence of female interest in politics may be the result of no questions of this nature being put to them.

It might also be suggested that women would follow the lead of their husbands in those times, in terms of voting preferences. The lives of most of the case-study sample were, in any case, so consumed with the sheer necessities of providing for their families, that very little energy would be expendable upon such "distant" matters as Government in Tasmania, let alone upon the mainland.

From the material so far collected in this study, the conclusion would have to be drawn that politics and feminist politics were concepts alien to the lives of most rural women in the Huon and Channel in the years 1900 to at least after World War II. One woman (Case Study 72) has pointed out that her grandmother considered herself a suffragette so in this instance the political changes were upheld. Obviously, the results of overseas political decisions such as wars and Depression did impact directly upon them, but these were accepted as facts of life rather than something which might be changed by political agitation.

4.5 Skill sets

Table 2 on page 61 shows a list of the skills which women, in the early years covered by this study, have talked of acquiring. As the table shows the list is multi-faceted and comprehensive. The women had undertaken these tasks since childhood or had stood beside their mother watching and learning the skills. A somewhat sanguine picture of their lives is painted by Garnsey (1944). In this author's view, women were content to take on the most daunting of tasks such as those listed in the table, as well as helping their husbands in the forests. Perhaps the truth is less romantic. In the absence of their husbands and to protect their children and the property the woman had no choice but to shoulder these burdens. They prided themselves on their skills "All through my life I was good with a rifle...and have always carried it with me and I have shot a lot of snakes." (Lowe 1994: 43).

The need to exercise these skills did not disappear with the appearance of more modern technologies as the twentieth century progressed. For rural women in the period towards the end of the century and into the twenty- first century some of the skills listed would still be relevant. One woman (Case 62) while talking to me reviewed Table 2 and said that, at a pinch, she thought she could carry out any of the tasks. She had never married and was accustomed to running her own property. Admittedly she did not keep pigs and would no longer consider it correct or legal to shoot raptors, wildlife or snakes. Social mores change. However, for those on farms or a small acreage, there are still chores that a townswoman might baulk at. Slaughtering unwanted cockerels may still be a task to be undertaken. An absence of readily available help in maintenance tasks in remoter areas must lead to a certain degree of self-sufficiency. This coupled to the fact that, for at least two of the women I interviewed, both partners were employed at a distance from the property and so both had to pitch in when required with any work to be done.

Table 2: Skills set for women in the early years of the study period

Farm Skills	Domestic Skills	Career Skills
Dairy Maid	Cook on Woodstove or Open Fire	Run a Shop
Butter Churner and Marketer	Bread Maker	Run a Post office
Cream Maker and Marketer	Jam and Preserve Maker	Telephonist
Horsewoman	Laundress with no running water	Book Keeper
Truck and car driver	Midwife	Ambulance Driver
Chicken Farmer	Family doctor or nurse	Church worker
Pig farmer/slaughterer	Carer for the elderly	Musician
Butcher	Seamstress/dressmaker	Army nurse
Snake Shooter	Knitter/crocheter	
Raptor/wildlife shooter	Piano player	
Tree feller		

Crosscut saw operator		
Tree stump remover		
Berry Farmer and picker		
Apple picker		
Apple packer and grader		

Chapter 5: "Modern" convenience

5.1 Running water on tap

Carrying buckets of water from a stream or well to supply the house was back breaking. For homes in Nicholls Rivulet, for example, water was still being carried in from an outdoor tank and heated in kerosene buckets on the fire in the 1950s (Case 69). The building of a reservoir up in the hills to supply Cygnet and the construction of a pipeline led to the "luxury" of running water on tap (Case 69).

5.2 Electricity

> *"We thought we were made when the power came on." (Watson 1987: 42)*

The coming of electricity brought welcome changes. Gardam quotes a description of the events leading to the power being ceremoniously switched on at Middleton. Flowerpot and Gordon were connected, along with Middleton on May 14th, 1930 due to the efforts of the Progress Association.

> *"By 8.30pm visitors from as far afield as Hobart and Kingston, as well as almost every local inhabitant, had gathered in the Middleton Hall. Dozens of red, green and cream lights festooned the hall, hanging from the walls and ceiling and set among the man-ferns decorating the stage. Red and white streamers added to the décor of the newly painted cream and green hall. The hall was, as usual, lit by lamps as it always had been for earlier socials and dances. It was converted into a "fairy bower" when the then Premier, J.C. McPhee, switched on the lights to prolonged and loud applause."(Gardam undated: 95).*

However, electricity and the changes it brought came slowly. People who did not live on the main road had to wait for years for connection. Power had been connected at Kettering in 1924. In Snug the town had electricity but had to wait till the 1950s to have a water supply connected (Gardam 2007: 128). In the Huon, electricity came to the main parts of Cygnet in 1923 and then the line was extended to Huonville and Franklin in 1926 (Burton undated, p.20). One of the women tells of being at school in Cygnet. Her family must have lived in an outlying area, for the story is set in the 1930s. The children rushed home that night, after a day of anticipation at school, because they knew that when they got home the power would be connected to their house. The family went out and bought a radio, despite their neighbour's predictions of financial ruin (Cygnet Living History Museum Oral History Folder number 1, CLH 00218).

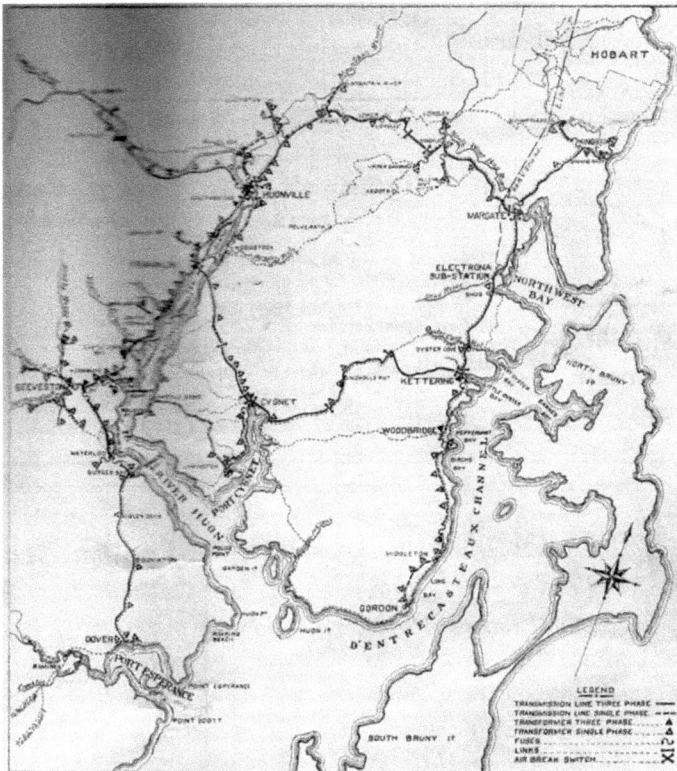

MAP SHOWING HIGH TENSION TRANSMISSION WIRES THROUGHOUT HUON DISTRICT.

Electricity supplies to the Huon (Huon Newspaper Co.1936)

The photograph shows a refrigerator from the 1930s or 1940s. This modern marvel replaced the old meat safe of the type shown on page 57. Photograph by the author from the collection at the "Apple Museum" at Grove in the Huon Valley 10/07/2012.

The woman in Case 28 rejoiced in her new washing machine. She and her husband had brought it back with them after a trip to Sydney. The washer-woman who had previously been employed to do the washing was unimpressed as she lost her job (Watson 1987: 22). In the 1950s the woman in Case 69 tells how proud she felt that her family had a washing machine (a single tub with a rubber wringer) because not too many people around had these. Another woman (Case 71) remembers the Home Arts teacher in High School in the early 1970s assuming that all the girls' homes would have a washing machine. She says that she sat very silent at the back of the class, unwilling to admit that her mother still washed in the twin sinks and used the copper boiler. Her mother eventually updated to a machine like the one described above. The woman in Case 71 lived for a number of years in a "shed" on the property while she and her husband built their home. They had a wood fired stove for cooking and heating. She describes using a generator for the first eighteen months to provide power. If the generator fuel ran out during the evening they simply gave up what they were doing and went to bed. When the generator was refuelled in the morning then she says "everything cranked up again" (Interview 2013).

Even though few had any electrical gadgets there was a rush to get power connected. After a lifetime of kerosene lamps and candles, washing tubs and camp ovens, it is not hard to see why this should be so. Along with electricity came the luxury of radio. One of the women tells of listening to the serials (Lowe 1994: 30). With this new technology in place a rapid connection to the wider world was established.

To women used to running their homes, cooking on open fires, doing washing in the outdoors and sewing by lamplight, the advent of electric power had immediate advantages. For many families, however, there was a long wait for connection to occur and purchase of labour saving devices depended upon having the means to buy them. Money was as always, for many of the women, in short supply. The wonders of "modern" living might be seen and coveted but the reality was that life in the home and on the farm continued for many years much as it had done in the past.

5.3 Motorised transport

By the 1920s the motor car had made its appearance in the Huon and the Channel. To make this new conveyance practical, roads were improved. For many households, however, the resurfacing of the roads from gravel to bitumen did not take place till the 1950s and 1960s (Interviews; Cases 64 and 69). Indeed today, in 2012, many country property owners and small communities in the Huon and Channel have to travel over "dirt" roads to reach their homes. At Abels Bay, an hour's drive from the State capital Hobart, for example, the road from Deep Bay starts as bitumen, but this peters out after a few kilometres so that the rest of the road past the settlement is pot-holed gravel until the road emerges at Eggs and Bacon Bay. This example would be one of many.

Garage in Huonville 1930s. From "Centenary of the Settlement of the Huon"
("Huon News" 1936)

Taking to the new freedoms offered, women learned to drive cars
and trucks. The husband of one of the women (Case 7) bought his
first Chevrolet truck in 1928 and his daughters became the first women
in the district to learn to drive (Lowe undated: 116). Another young
woman learned to drive in 1928 because her father was unable to do
so (Lowe 1994: 28). Yet another, (Case 16), was injured after falling
from her bicycle and learned to drive. She would drive her children to
the movies in Woodbridge (Lowe 1994: 126). During the years of the
Second World War the woman in Case 14 made good use of her
driving skills, taking the Chevrolet truck up to Hobart two or three
times a week to deliver fruit. Her husband had joined the army and
was away from home. After delivering the fruit she would collect ten
or fifteen people coming to work as fruit pickers and drive them back
to Snug Falls (Lowe 1994: 44).

Buses were running from Cygnet to Hobart by 1924. Further
services came into place in 1935 (Cockerill 1987: 12). A "picture bus"
ran in the thirties from Woodbridge on Friday nights, leaving for
Hobart at 6pm and returning from Hobart at 11pm. The return fare
was 60cents.

For married women, as for their single sisters, community festivities
provided a welcome break in routine. When motor cars had become
more common the whole family could join in the outing. O'Malley

(2009: 57) tells of his mother's delight at being taken to a monthly dance in the Huon Valley. He says she was never short of partners because she was a good dancer, but his Dad preferred to talk to his mates or play cards outside. However, whether or not he enjoyed dancing, the dutiful husband always had the last few dances with his wife. Tots and babies were made up beds on the bench seats round the hall and the older kids went and slept in the cars if they became too tired.

Other stories apart from O'Malley (2009) tell of family picnics to the Channel coast and of regattas on the Huon, days of festivity and enjoyment for the women. Annual regattas continued at Shipwright's Point until the 1960s, having been held there each year since 1863 (Hayes. In Hammond, 2004, p.49). In the very early years the steamers would bring guests down from Hobart and in the 1930s one of the women in this study writes that the distant sighting of the Hobart steamer would be the cue for the locals to put the potatoes and peas on to cook for the crowds (Hayes. In Hammond 2004: 49).

Chapter 6: Working on the land

6.1 Farm and orchard work

"Sometimes a hail storm would wipe out the whole crop within minutes and a whole year's work. Sometimes we could sell the damaged fruit for juice—or it was left on the trees, or dumped, or fed to the livestock. This happened sometimes three or four years in succession. Eventually the orchards came out in the district. The farmers couldn't pay wages, buy manure or buy sprays for next year. Sometimes when the apples were sent overseas a bill would come back." (Lowe 1994: 29).

For the women whose working lives revolved round their home and property, they shared with their husbands the uncertainties of work on the land. Especially at harvest time, in the orchards and berry fields, working days went from early morning to late at night to make ends meet. Inside work in the house would be done, then the woman would join her husband on the outdoor tasks of picking, then packing. She might label the apple cases he was working to make. If things went wrong after shipment, the only return might be a bill for fifty or seventy pounds owed to the shippers (Watson 1987: 44). These outside events caused by wars and the Depression were far beyond the control of the families, as were the tricks played by nature.

The woman in Case 21 is said to have calculated that when she came to live in Snug as a young girl in the early 1920s there were thirty small orchards around the settlement. The orchards were on the lower ground with berry fruits grown up towards the Snug Tiers (Gardam 2007: 107).

Often their menfolk would have to leave the property looking for another source of income to tide the family over hard times. They returned to the bush to fell timber, worked on roads or took work at the Carbide Factory. Then the wife would roll up her sleeves and manage alone or with the help of the children. If she was physically strong enough she might continue with clearing the land for planting, grubbing out tree stumps and moving felled timber. She would take over the slaughter of the pig for meat, carry a rifle around with her to shoot snakes and predators and generally do what needed to be done to the best of her ability (Lowe 1994: 44).

To buy the properties, loans were taken out, furniture might be sold. These loans had to be repaid. For many of the families this was a struggle—which might be lost. For the woman in Case 4, her life changed when her father injured his hip and could not work so could not meet mortgage payments. The mortgage was foreclosed and the family had to leave the property. (O'Rourke 2008: 5).

When harvest time came around families from outside the area would move in to stay in the pickers' huts and supplement the local labour force. In the early days, however, people could quite easily make a living from their small orchards as long as they kept a cow and raised a pig for meat. A case of apples would be sold for six or seven shillings in these days but there was no great pressure to meet selling deadlines and expenses were lower (Watson 1987: 20). As the orchards expanded and more and more fruit was shipped overseas, so complications multiplied. Shipping was a perennial problem.

Pickers' huts would sleep up to eight members of a family, accomodated in two small areas divided from the central space. The beds were slatted wooden bunks, four in each area. The living area would contain a fireplace and a table. Cooking might be done on the fire or in the open around the huts. During the Second World War the huts became home to Italian prisoners of war who apparently found the high country in the Snug Tiers similar to their far-away homes. Their stay there is remembered for their love of music and their playing and singing after work.

A restored pickers' hut at Hartzview is shown in the photographs on the next page. Hartzview gave up growing soft fruit and now has a successful vineyard with a popular restaurant. The photographs were taken by the author and is used with the permission of the owners of Hartzview, July 2012.

Restored pickers' hut at Hartzview, 2012

Restored pickers' hut at Hartzview, 2012

In 1930 a Royal Commission was appointed to inquire into and report as to "certain matters relating to the marketing of Tasmanian apples and pears." (Borchardt 1960). The report dealt with the methods of shipping fruit, for example the allocation of space and the carryover of fruit during the season. The Commission found that dissatisfaction felt by growers was due to four main causes.

1. Distance of the market, difficulties in shipping two and a half to three million cases of apples and pears on as many as forty two steamers within four or five months of the year.
2. Export of fruit not suitable for the overseas market.
3. The unbusiness-like ways of the growers.
4. Certain defects in the procedures and methods at present followed.

To remedy these matters it was recommended that the "Fresh Fruits Overseas Marketing Act." (1927) be followed. More State control as in New Zealand was advocated. Better inspection should be undertaken of fruit destined for overseas markets.

Watson (1987), in the introduction to "Full and Plenty" comments that in 1987 "There is a huge gulf between the Huon growers and the people who service their industry. Hobart waterside workers cop most of the blame for the industry's ills."

It would be hard to fail to understand the frustration, anger and eventual despair of many of those families. While expanding the orchards held the promise of greater income, not only nature, but external economic events such as the Great Depression crashed into their labour intensive life-style and left them struggling. The problems were those of scale. No longer could an easy living be made from a smallholding as long as the family had a cow and a pig.

6.2 Alternative sources of income

The coming of industry to the Channel in the form of the Carbide Works at Electrona provided an alternative source of income for men. Still, working the land was an ingrained tradition and the men would return to this after shifts at the factory. Despite all the difficulties and setbacks, and even when the menfolk were trying to combine factory work with farming, there is a description from one of the women of the days spent picking raspberries and hops which speaks of "happy days filled with laughter and singing" (Lowe 1994: 50).

The Channel communities were in some respects more fortunate than those in the upper Huon because of their proximity to the sea. There was a scallop industry in the D'Entrecasteaux Channel from around 1920 (Perrin and Hay 1987) which provided some employment when fruit picking was over for the year.

Berry pickers at Hartzview in the mid twentieth century. Photograph from the records held at Hartzview Vineyard.

The scallop season lasted for three months. At first two boats were operating. By 1924 there were several boats (Perrin and Hay 1987). The fishery had problems relating to a sustainable catch and was closed in 1930 and 1931, then again partially closed in 1964 (Perrin and Hay 1987). Demand increased and there was increased production in the 1940s, during the Second World War. At this time the woman in Case 74 was a child and stood beside her mother in the scallop sheds. By 1949 catches had decreased markedly. In the 1960s new types of dredges were tried out, described by the woman in Case 74 as having a saw-toothed blade to scrape up the scallops. The results were devastating for the fishery in the Channel with the beds destroyed. Also in the Channel men might find work boatbuilding. A factory making sassafras clothes pegs operated for a time. However, the backbone of work and lifestyle remained firmly tied to working the land.

The quotation earlier in this chapter seems an appropriate way to discuss on life on the land. There were many instances of hardship, disappointment and struggle. The women in the study worked from their earliest years with their families, then married and took up the burden once more in setting up new homes, new properties. They worked while pregnant, gave birth, often at home with the local midwife in attendance. After the births they worked around feeding and raising their family. The enterprise of farming and all their labour might be wasted in an hour's hailstorm. The hopes of an income could be dashed by events overseas beyond their control. Eventually farms might be sold.

Through all this, in the stories of their social life, their home entertainment and jokes, of laughter and singing in the berry fields, there is a thread of courage and endurance. To wrap a cow-pat in newspaper as a birthday present each year and to, no doubt, laugh with the recipient who knew very well what the parcel would contain; to serenade your wife as she toiled beside you shows, at least in my eyes, an indomitable spirit.

6.3 Apple growing as an industry

Towards the middle of the twentieth century, according to the foreword by Humphrey McQueen in "Full and Plenty" (Watson 1987), apple growing had become an industry, like motor cars or tin cans. Strife on the wharves in Melbourne and Sydney in the 1920s saw congestion on the Hobart wharves during the apple season. Port Huon came into use with a first direct shipment to the UK in 1929 (Townsley 1991: 286).

An apple ship at Port Huon. Photograph from a collection owned by Steve Lucas.

McQueen in Watson(1987) notes that capital stock in the orchards had to be renewed every twenty five to thirty years.

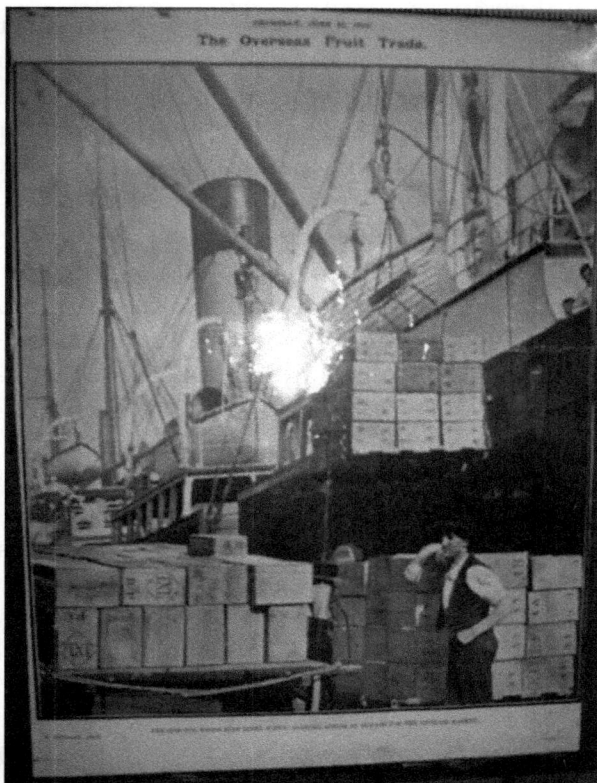

The S.S. Argyllshire moored and loading at Port Huon in 1932. This photograph is found on the walls of the antique shop at the "Margate Train" complex. According to the caption the ship was a vessel trading for the Scottish Shire Line, weighing 11,916 tons and was 526 feet long. The ship was loading 69,662 cases of apples.

This meant that each producer had to assess what demand would be in decades to come. Fashions in fruit changed, keeping qualities might outweigh sweetness and appearance might outweigh taste. Artificial fertilizers and chemical sprays were commonly used. Fruit had to be a standardised size. Orchardists were at the receiving end of these changes. Shopping patterns were changing with the closure of corner stores. The world of biotechnology and monoculture production had arrived. The primary producers blamed the bureaucrats, the trade unions and the shipping firms for the difficulties these changes caused to their way of life.

A woman from the Huon, (Case 58), describes her work after marriage in an atmosphere more of a factory than a family business. At first she went out picking around Huonville in the early mornings with fog and frost all around and the apple crop wet in her hands. For this work she was paid by the day. She was lucky enough to move to the packing sheds where she worked under contract on eight hour shifts. A worker could earn $20 to $25 for packing one hundred cases. At the beginning she could only pack 24 cases a day but worked up to 50 or 60. The working week was Monday to Friday and on Saturday mornings. She hired a young girl to come in to cook and to look after the children.

She describes having to wrap each apple and notes that during the Second World War the wrapping paper was thick and coarse, like newsprint. Working to be paid by the case, it is easy to see how this unmanageable paper slowed down production and was most unpopular with the packers. She describes how four workers were placed on each side of the rotary bin grader. They changed position every two hours to allow each person to have a turn at packing the bigger apples which, of course took less time and so increased individual output. With what she and her husband earned they were able to build their house. She describes factory work as reasonable. The bosses did not appreciate slacking off, but you could chat and have a bit of fun (Watson 1987: 71).

The old way of picking hops in early 1900's
Photograph provided by Madge Lowe (Margate)

Another woman (Case 64) describes going to work in the cannery office in Cygnet. At weekends she would go to work in the packing sheds and could make more money there for her weekend's work than she was paid for office work. In the 1950s apples were still being grown around Cygnet and sent for sale to Hobart (Case69).

Another, less common crop, especially at Brookfield near Margate on the Channel was the growing of hops. Again women were to the fore at harvest time. Like the story of the apple industry, the hop fields at Brookfield became unprofitable and the industry closed down in the mid-1970s. Several generations of the Lowe family managed the property which also ran cattle and sheep. The hop crop for 1975 could not be sold and was stockpiled, ending seven decades of production. The property then concentrated on its cattle and lamb markets. Later vineyards were planted.

Bullock team with a farmer and his daughter and grandson at Glen Huon. (Photograph taken from a calendar published by the Upper Huon History Group, 2012.)

By the middle of the twentieth century mechanisation had come to farming properties with tractors making an appearance on the land. Many farmers resisted this change preferring to continue with their working horses. The photograph above must be taken in the 1920s or 30s judging by the woman's dress. Her father was still working a bullock team. As late as the 1950s the farm horse was still used in the orchards around Cygnet and the woman in Case 69 tells of the excitement when the family bought a tractor. She would ride down the road in the trailer and feel like royalty.

Ploughing the orchard. Photograph from the collection of Steve Lucas.

Apple grader. Photo taken by author from collection at the Apple Museum at Grove 10/7/12.

Chapter 7: The effects of wars and the Great Depression

7.1 World War I

> *"The Anzac story has endured and become the main story, often the only story, of the First World War.......... This has obscured other views, including the story of women in the war, both overseas (about eighty Tasmanian nurses served in the theatres of war) and on the home front. Less enduring has been the memory of grief, of young lives shattered, of families broken and distraught for years..." (Henning 2008)*

Men from the lower Channel who enlisted to serve in WWI. With permission from the Southern Channel Progress Association files.

In 1914 the First World War broke out in Europe. Paul Kelly (2001) describes the ties of kinship and loyalty to the Empire which led to Australia's entry into that war.

One of the consequences of this war was that Germans living in Australia were sent to internment camps. Censorship and surveillance increased and were resented by many. Social fractures appeared resulting in the bitterly contested and unsuccessful conscription referendums held in 1916 and 1917. In this debate polarisation occurred between middle and working class communities. By 1916 enthusiasm for the war had waned to such an extent that a huge rally held in Melbourne Town Hall brought forward only twelve men willing to volunteer (McAlman 1993, p.89). In the referenda, according to Townsley (1991: 273) the returns for Port Cygnet supported the No argument, while in Huonville the Yes case received strong support.

It may seem strange seen from the vantage point of the present day that, given that many of their grandfathers and great grandfathers, their grandmothers and great grandmothers had been dumped unceremoniously on the shores of Tasmania as convicts, loyalty to the British Empire was still strong in the south of the State. A convict heritage was hidden in the efforts to attain respectability in the community, but in such a small area the antecedents of families must have been well known. Never-the-less, the British Empire represented ties to a far-away homeland and when the call went out for volunteers, men enlisted in what was seen as a great adventure. Many were very young, some still in their teens.

Of the 15,485 men who enlisted in Tasmania, two thirds enlisted in the first two years of the war. Two thousand, four hundred and thirty two men were killed. A letter written from army headquarters to one of the families in the Channel speaks to the sadness of loss. A mother has written trying to find out more details of her son's death. The letter in the files of the South Channel Progress Association shows that, in reply, an official writes that "In the very heavy fighting at Pozieres, a number of our men were reported "missing", as in the absence of definite evidence that they had been killed in action, there was a possibility that they had been taken prisoner by the Germans." The letter continues with the news that as no reports of the men's survival had been received this slight hope had now ended. A Court of Inquiry had pronounced them killed in action. The irony is that this news was received three months before the end of World War I. Many more men returned broken in health. Memorials in the small communities of the Huon and Channel and on remote country beach fronts testify to the losses sustained.

In Oyster Cove the population was one hundred and twenty five. Eight men from that small community enlisted and all came home safely. At nearby Kettering, with a population of two hundred and twenty five, eleven men enlisted. Eight of these men were killed (Gardam 2005: 143) In Judbury, four sons of the Bond family went to war. Only one, the youngest, came home. When the Honour Roll was unveiled at the school, the school teacher had taught all but one of the young men whose names were inscribed there (Woolley 20002: 213). The Ranelagh Soldiers' Memorial Hall has Honour Boards which give the names of eight former students from Huonville School and 25 names from Lucaston. Those in Glen Huon tell a similar story. For such small communities, dependent on manpower for survival, those losses would have been devastating.

In remote corners of the Huon and Channel small monuments attest to the losses the communities suffered. This plaque at Randal's Bay commemorates the fallen. The great branches of the pine trees which sweep down over the memorial come from trees planted as an original memorial before the plaque was erected.
Photograph by the author (2013).

One of the women from Cygnet tells of this sense of devastation

(O'Rourke 2008: 128). By 1915 there had been little news of the progress of the war. The newspapers were limited in what they could publish and there was no other means of obtaining news. Only when she attended a Red Cross meeting in Cygnet did the extent of the horror of what was happening, first in the Dardanelles, then in Palestine and in the trenches of Flanders hit home. Before long, lists of those killed and injured did begin to appear in the papers. Among the names were those of her dancing partners and young men she had bid farewell to only weeks before. The effect upon her left her unable to take part in social festivities. She says that she did the work that needed to be done, went to church and nothing else.

Of those who did return, many were scarred mentally and physically by suffering and by the horrors they had seen. Heart problems occurred (Watson 1987: 21) and lingering effects of gas attacks (Lowe 1994: 89). Those at home probably heard little of these horrors. Letters would minimise the hardships to protect family. A brother writing to his sister in Queensland from Gallipoli is laconic. He and his brother are sharing a nice dug-out which is just big enough for them both, with a bit of a fireplace cut into the sap. He is practicing his cooking skills, which are improving[1].

A common experience was that even after their return the men could not talk to their families, but only amongst those who had served alongside them in the forces. The absence of the young men sent to war was noted particularly in farming areas like the Huon and Channel. The women left behind had to step in and take over the work which had to be done. Then, when the men who returned were damaged physically and mentally, again the women of the families had to cope with these difficulties.

7.2 On the Home Front

"A pet goat belonging to one of Herbert Skinner's daughters was auctioned to support Belgium." (Woolley 2002: 305)

It is noted by Woolley (2002) that the goat was returned to the child after the raffle. Women banded together under the auspices of the Red Cross to sew and knit for the troops. The Glen Huon circle

---

[1] Letter from Gallipoli held by Mrs. J. Amos in Cygnet.

contributed "21 shirts, 51 pairs of flannel pants, 38 pairs of knitted socks, 100 pairs of slippers, 7 knitted balaclavas, 3 mufflers, 9 pairs of mittens, 9 pairs of bed socks, 10 knitted eye bandages" (Woolley 2002: 305). Similar contributions were made by the branch at Woodbridge according to the "Mercury" in 1916. In addition to their contribution of comforts for the troops, the women also organized fund raising events, for example balls.

7.3 After the war

"They had this war service scheme to put men on the land, but it was a terrific mistake. My brother went around to visit the different orchards and places where men had been settled, but they were raw: they were not in any way used to orcharding work. They were put on these tracts of land and told the apples would grow and they would make a living. They were sadly disillusioned because they just couldn't do the work." (Watson 1987: 21)

The effects of war upon the returned soldiers have already been discussed. This had been touted as "The War to end all wars." Promises were made to treat those who survived as heroes.

When the troops came back to Australia land grants were made under the term "Soldier Settlements". These were a disastrous mistake in many cases when the men brought in had no knowledge of the work they were expected to undertake. Failure and disillusionment followed, compounded by the disenchantment already experienced by the standard of leadership during the war. According to Beresford (1983: 91) one thousand, nine hundred and seventy six grants were made in Tasmania. By 1929 seven hundred and seventy seven of the recipients were still on their land—a total of 39% and a melancholy catalogue of failure. These figures are taken by Beresford from the Commonwealth Parliamentary Papers, Volume II, 1929.

All this exacerbated the already fragile mental health of returning soldiers. Such was the public unease that a Royal Commission was established into the administration of the Soldier Settlement Department.

A summary of its findings was published in "The Mercury" on 30/09/1926.

"The frequent failure of returned soldiers to make a success of farming caused public alarm and the Royal Commission was set up to investigate the causes. The Commission found that the lack of suitable criteria of selection had led to the settlement of men on the land who could not possibly succeed...

The inability of the Minister to enforce a strict administration of the business side of settlements—an inability based on political and humane reasons—caused the scheme to fall to pieces." (Borchardt 1960: 36).

Also, following the disastrous years of war came an influenza pandemic—the so-called "Spanish 'Flu". Tasmania in 1919 was the last state in Australia to experience the outbreak of pneumonic influenza. The word of this "plague" had already reached the island, along with horrific statistics of the deaths it had caused throughout the world. The island prepared for the worst with Claremont Army Base being turned into a hospital (Beresford 1982: 108). The "Tasmanian Mail" of August 21st, 1919 noted that Church Services were to be held outdoors to minimise infection and attendees were to keep a distance of three feet from their nearest neighbour (information taken from "The Channel: All Areas". File Cha. 1, Channel Heritage Museum). The reason for this precaution and others, such as the wearing of face masks, was obvious. The illness itself varied in severity but pneumonia was known to be a complication. In a seven week period one hundred and seventy one people were known to have died in Tasmania. This statistic, however, only accounts for those who were registered hospital patients. The true toll may well be greater (Beresford 1982: 110).

7.4 The Great Depression

"Times in the late twenties and thirties were hard: people who talk about the hard times in the nineteen eighties don't know what they were like then."(O'Rourke 2008: 191)

Economic times in Tasmania had been hard throughout the 1920s. Townsley (1991: 283) points out that "Tasmania knew economic depression for years before the Wall Street crash." The Great Depression worldwide only amplified these difficulties. Telling of her life in Northern Tasmania, "Marjorie" remembers lighting fires along the three mile walk to school just to get warm. On her feet she wore thin slippers with cardboard soles. She says that the family had no social life such as Church because they didn't have anything to dress in. She gave up on school when she was thirteen because they did not have enough money for the few things the school required. Working at home, she was able to wear men's old clothing and boots. (Lowenstein 1978: 41).

The women in this study were accustomed to lives of thrift and frugality. In these hardened circumstances, their rural lifestyle to some extent mitigated the oncoming disaster. Where on the mainland, in areas such as Richmond in Melbourne, households might be reduced to penury and have to pawn their last assets if a family member became ill (McAlman 1993: 151), at least in rural southern Tasmania food was still available. In Hobart, clothes might be stolen from the clothesline and vegetables from the back garden to feed starving children. In the country, milk from the cow, meat from rabbits and the pig and butter from the churned milk could be put on the table. Mothers were accustomed to baking bread and making jam from the berries in the fields.

The women made do and mended, as women before them had done in times of trouble. They could make rugs for the floor by cutting strips from old garments, then sorting them by colour and knotting them through hessian to form a rag rug. Needlecraft books supplied patterns for re-using cotton frocks by dyeing them and cutting them down for children's dresses, and outworn adults' combinations could become a child's vest (McLeod 2005: 219,220and 226).

To women accustomed to making their own clothes and to converting anything salvageable into something smaller for a child, these thrifty ideas were not novel. One of the women in the study was quite proud of the unbleached flour bag knickers her mother made for her, with their coloured crochet edges (Lowe undated: 36). Clothes might be worn and patched, aprons and knickers might be made from sugar bags or flour bags and curtains from hessian, but no one starved and, again in contrast to other places, only one of the women speaks of losing a property (O'Rourke 2008: 191). Her account tells of crops which could not be sold and had to be dumped as there were no buyers with money to spend. One man (Watson 1987: 34) remembers the frustration of external events costing him all his savings when the General Strike in England in 1926 left his apples rotting on the wharves.

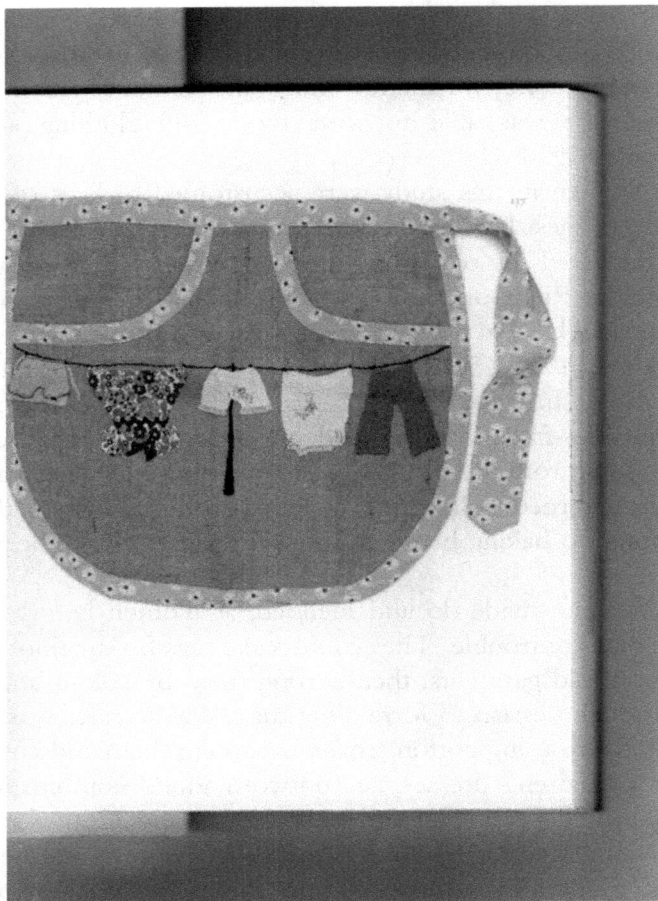

Decorated apron made from hessian and fabric scraps (McLeod, 2005)

The economic onslaught of the Great Depression dismayed even the most stoic. The naked hardships felt in the cities were mitigated by the self-sufficiency of rural life, but the ownership of properties was under threat. When crops could not be sold, men in the family often had to look for additional work away from their farms and orchards to augment their income. The women were left to contribute extra labour and to supplement income by selling produce, such as butter and cream. This income would pay for those grocery items, like tea and sugar, which had to be bought. Having made a decision to join family in New Zealand (a decision thwarted by the failure of the apple agent's business in Hobart) the woman whose property was lost saw her husband return to timber felling, leaving her with the farm. He would return home on a Saturday and would have to row back across the Huon on the Sunday to return to this work (O'Rourke 2008: 34).

Another woman in the Channel would take one end of a cross-cut saw, while her two sons worked the other end, to cut firewood. They then carried this out of the bush to the roadside to sell. Sometimes this hard-won wood was stolen (Lowe 1994: 33). Yet another picked blackberries to sell for extra money, while her husband grew a berry crop to supplement his work making apple cases (Lowe undated: 37). This man made five pence for each case he put together and also sold firewood by the roadside. In the Channel a factory making clothes pegs from sassafras wood was set up and provided an extra income until the wood supply ran out (Gardam 2005: 141). Even in the Huon, men went from place to place hoping to find a day's work. This would be the period, described in an earlier quotation, when householders might leave the door off the latch so that these wanderers could claim shelter for a night.

7.5 The Second World War

"We had Italian prisoners of war at Nicholls Rivulet. My brother-in-law's, there were three or four there. He had them in a camp and they worked for him and they did some of the most marvellous concrete work. He's got a path down from his house….all coloured cement." (Cygnet Living History Museum: Oral History Folder 8 C.L.H.-0025)

In the same way that this Second World War followed its predecessor internationally and came hard upon the heels of the Great Depression, so having to face a world- wide conflict again hit hard upon the families in the Huon and Channel District. This war differed from that of 1914/1918 in that the threat of invasion came close to Australian shores. The reality that was faced was that Australia had a population of around seven million people. This population was concentrated in the southernmost parts of the continent. They lived on a huge and largely empty land mass which was almost impossible to defend against the threat of invasion by superior forces (Townsley 1991: 429).

The men and women who served in war did not always travel far overseas. War came to the Pacific. Bombs fell on Darwin in 1942.

Mini-submarines from Japan were threatening Sydney harbour. The fear of invasion reached the shores of the Huon and the Channel. A single bomb shelter appeared in the Sandfly area (Lowe undated: 66). An air raid shelter was dug in Franklin Square in Hobart. Hobart citizens were issued with gas masks (Lowe undated: 66). Plans for a "scorched earth" policy in the event of invasion were apparently in place. (Cygnet Living History Museum Oral History Folder 8, C.L.H.-0025).

The woman telling this story (Case 57) believed that her family would be given orders to abandon their home, setting fire to the building (though she puzzled over who would do this) and to take to the hills with little or nothing. She believed they would be ordered to leave the sick and elderly behind. I have, so far, been unable to discover a document such as she describes, but certainly in March 1942 "The Mercury" newspaper in Hobart was discussing civilian involvement in a "scorched earth" policy in the event of invasion. Under orders from the State Authority cars, lorries, motor cycles and pedal cycles would have to be destroyed, along with small boats. (www.nla.gov.au "Trove")

In this war women played a more active role in the armed services. Some were stationed mainly in Australia, but nurses were sent to serve on the front line. Others took on "traditional" male roles, working in factories and delivering mail. Both men and women trained as Air Raid Precaution Wardens. Women took the role of taxi drivers, tram drivers and conductors and worked as mechanics. They drove ambulances and heavy trucks (Lowe, undated, p.66). In the case of the woman (Case 60) who grew up in the far south of the State, she and her brothers and sisters stepped in to assist their father keep his sawmill running. She became a "left handed tree feller" (Interview, 19/6/12), climbing up steps, driven into the tree trunk to a platform, to fell the tree. She was in her teens. Her sister learned to fire the steam boiler in the forest with their father supervising. An older sister had studied secretarial work and book keeping and managed the mill accounts.

The Red Cross once again began efforts to raise money for the troops. Canteens were opened, food parcels collected and sent. Clothing was once again made for the armed forces (C.W.A. Tasmania 1996: 12). In the Country Women's Association the war effort was supported by sending food parcels to Britain until rationing ended there. Funds were raised for the Australian Comforts Fund, for Red Cross work, for the support of prisoners of war, Air Raid Relief for Britain and Chinese Relief. In Hobart, the City Hall became a depot for assembling camouflage nets. The nets were twenty four feet square. They were sent from small towns and country districts to be finished in Hobart and from there dispatched to the armed forces. On an average, eighty women a day worked at the City Hall completing one hundred nets a day (C.W.A. Tasmania 1996: 12).

Now resident in Cygnet, Mrs Janice Amos has records kept by her mother of the work done by local women's organisations in Queensland during the Second World War. I mention this to illustrate not only the type of work undertaken in such organisations but the more laughable events which occurred in the course of this work. The Queensland group in question had been requested to sew undergarments for the troops. A pattern was provided which involved sewing tucks into the material in underpants where it joined the waistband. Some of the volunteer seamstresses were having difficulty in fitting these tucks. The women conferred and it was suggested that gathers rather than tucks would be an easier method. Correspondence ensued as the matter of the underpants was discussed at Army Headquarters. A final ruling came back to the working group that tucks should continue to be used, as gathers might provide shelter for vermin. By the time the decision was reached there was no longer any need for underpants to be sewn.

During the Second World War, Red Cross volunteers in the Channel ran balls, held competitions for the crown of "Miss Red Cross" and every June held fairs at Woodbridge School to raise funds for the War effort. Few of the women mention volunteering but it can be assumed that they went to the balls, to gala events and patronised the annual fair. While community organisations such as the CWA were active from 1936, and earlier temperance associations (Alexander 1991) took up the attention of women, the lives of most of the women in this study were so centred on home and family land that there is little record of their involvement in other activities.

Also, during the Second World War a women's organization which came to be known as the Women's Land Army was formed. Records show that women from this organisation served on farms and orchards in the Huon and Channel (Scott 1986). For the women in this study, however, working on the land and filling the place of men who were overseas on active duty was a normal part of daily life. In some cases Italian prisoners of war were sent to work alongside the farming population.

For the women in the Huon and the Channel the fact that men were again called upon to join the armed forces left them, as before, to take over the running of farms, orchards and shops. The women of the apple growing districts packed and picked the fruit, carted the harvest to the wharves and helped unload it there. Newly found driving skills were put to good use and, after delivery of fruit, the return journey would bring out the pickers on the back of the truck.

As part of air raid precautions, the woman in Case 12 records that her father walked the district every night to enforce the compulsory black-out and that trenches were dug for shelter in the grounds of Margate school (Lowe 1993: 28).

The lower huts at Hartzview which were home to Italian prisoners of war. Photo by researcher with permission from the owner of Hartzview Vineyard

The woman in Case 57 tells of the fear that gripped the civilian population with the perceived threat of invasion. Living at the time in Judbury, blackout blinds were part of everyday life. In the event of being ordered to leave their homes instructions were provided for the actions to be taken in case of invasion. A list was provided of essential items which should be taken, for example a mug and a spoon and fork and knife. (Cygnet Living History Museum, Oral history Folder 8

C.H.L.-2005). Tank traps were built at Longley with pillars and chains across the road (Watson, 1987, p.69), though a sceptic observed that the tanks would simply drive around these. Fortunately the threat of invasion receded so these dire plans never had to be put into operation.

Rationing came into force with coupons for food and clothing. As before, in war and Depression, the families on the land had means to sustain themselves, although new regulations meant this became more difficult. Most families were self-sufficient in vegetables, milk, fruit and eggs. An unofficial barter system operated to exchange goods. The police, however, checked on stock and crops. One woman notes that permission was required even to slaughter the family pig . Despite the difficulties in bartering, families still managed to trade eggs, butter and cream, vegetables and even fish with the local shopkeepers. Ration books were used as a last resort (Gardam 2005: 143).

The rationing of petrol for all but essential travel meant that the horse and cart were once again utilised as transport. For trucks a system of charcoal burners was installed to provide gas. This necessitated reloading the boiler at the top of the hill climb between Hobart and Huonville (Watson 1987: 69).

For the berry farmers the war brought some benefits. Their fruit was in demand in the jam factories which were working full out to provide jam for the American forces in the Pacific. Because berry fruit was an essential commodity the men were not available for military service (Gardam 2005: 141).

The same was not true for local orchards. There were few workers to pick the crop. As the war progressed it became difficult, if not impossible to ship apples overseas because of the scarcity of ships and the danger. Many orchards near Kettering were chopped out. Trial Bay near Kettering became a dumping ground for apples which could not be shipped. The stench from the rotting fruit filled the air (Lowe undated: 45).

The lack of shipping to transport apples abroad contributed to the decline of the steamers which plied the Channel. Road transport took over the task of taking apples to the wharves after the War. According to one of the women, during the War no fruit was allowed to be sold. Vehicles were inspected on the Huon Highway to ensure that no unauthorised apples were being carried. The Government of the day paid a levy for the crop which was then left unpicked or taken to be dumped.

One of the women in the study (Case 47) had some nursing training. She enlisted as a Voluntary Aid and left for an overseas posting on the 27/8/1941. This was the first experiment in sending women to serve alongside the army. This woman was sent to the Middle East (Lowe undated: 27).

Another (Case 21) also trained as a Voluntary Aid, but she was required to return home to care for the family (Lowe undated: 32). The woman in Case 40 worked as a civilian at the barracks in Hobart during the Second World War. She travelled home to the Channel at weekends by bus. She tells of being issued with a gas mask and being the only person on the bus carrying one. Her thought then was that she would be one of few survivors if Hobart was attacked (Lowe undated: 66).

The woman in Case 44 joined the V.A.D. when the Second World War broke out. She and other recruits slept on sacks filled with straw in the Hobart Show Grounds in the sheep pens! She drove an ambulance. After she married, her husband was serving overseas. The woman went back to help her father on the farm. She says that all the fruit and vegetables were commandeered by the Government and sent to the troops overseas. Her mother buried two shilling pieces under the floor of the house as a precaution against times getting worse, and they buried tins of food in the orchard. When her husband came home they applied for a Soldier's Settlement which helped them to buy their own farm.(Lowe undated: 66)

None of the women in the study tell of serving with the Australian Women's Land Army. This was their everyday work already. Scott does describe the experiences of one young woman sent to the orchards at Randall's Bay, nine miles from Cygnet. She tells of working with local women picking apples and pears and of her introduction to horse drawn sledges (Scott 1986: 81).

Unlike the dark days of the Depression when the hardship of the times weighed upon the lives of the women, the days of 1939 to 1945 pass in their stories with few comments unless they, or a family member, were closely involved. Losses in Tasmania were less than in the previous war with 1100 killed. Of these, several hundred were P.O.W.s taken captive by the Japanese. There seems little of the shock and horror that had been felt as casualties mounted in World War I. Perhaps the sufferings of earlier years had, to some extent at least, inured the communities to the strictures of rationing and the failure to get crops to market. As the Second World War progressed and the threat of invasion lessened, life in the Huon Valley and the Channel seems to have proceeded much as usual, complicated by the laws governing food rationing. Major changes, however, were to follow in the later years of the twentieth century.

Part 2: 1945 to 2013

Historic builings still feature in the landscape of the Huon and Channel.
Photograph by the author

Chapter 8: The Post War period (1945-1967)

8.1 Slowly changing times

"I wanted to join the army or the police force but my parents laughed at the idea so I got work in a shop in the town." (Case 69)

In the years immediately following the Second World War, life gradually returned to normal. Families bought new properties, one family selling furniture to make up a deposit on their farm (Lowe 1994: 97/98). In another case the couple were able to buy the family property (Watson 1987: 96). Marriages were entered into. In Case 19 the couple went on to have eight children (Lowe 1994: 100). In another case, the woman says that, immediately after her marriage in 1945, she was caught up in the family business, as every member of the family was involved in the orchards. When she had leisure she enjoyed sewing and knitting. The family still held sing-a-longs and she listened to their battery operated radio. The Red Cross organisation was active in the community along with the Girl Guide organisation and she found time to be involved in both. In Sandfly the woman in case 38 was a founding member of the local CWA branch (Lowe undated: 53/54). The apple shed work became more industrialised with the woman in Case 58 working eleven hour days from Monday till Friday and on Saturday mornings. (Watson 1987: 70/71)

Rationing of sugar continued until 1947 (according to recollections of the woman in Case 12). She notes that meat and clothing rationing was stopped in 1948, but that butter and petrol were still in restricted supply until 1950. Overseas shipping routes were re-established and trade was able to resume, though incidents overseas such as the closure of the Suez Canal during a localised war in 1956 meant ships carrying the apple crop were unable to reach their port of destination. Wars continued overseas, the undeclared so-called Cold War, war in Korea and war in Vietnam. This last war is mentioned by one of the women (Case 69), when she talks of a relative being called up for National Service which might have led to him serving in Vietnam with the Australian Army. Fortunately and after much worry to his family he was not conscripted.

Dressed for town. Hats and gloves in place. Phtographic collection of Steve Lucas

The woman in Case 73 was born just before the outbreak of WWII. Her story, of all the women I interviewed, most reflects the patterns which had been established in the preceding years. Her mother and father lived at the southern end of the Channel. The major difference in her story, from those I had already heard or learned about, was that her father owned a fishing boat and fished for scallops. Thus her mother, in addition to caring for the home and property, worked to help her husband in the scallop sheds. As a small child she stood beside her mother to learn the skills. Apart from this, her story is one which might well have taken place decades before.

Her father also owned a small portable sawmill. He milked the family cow and her mother made and sold butter. This butter was pressed into wooden moulds carved out with a thistle design so that the finished product was presented as a neat circular piece of butter with a raised thistle on top. I have seen this same design in Scotland as a child. They had berry fields and a small orchard.

She helped her mother work the butter separator, describing it to me as a container into which the milk was poured. Under this was a chamber with revolving small cup-like paddles. By turning a handle the chamber rotated, separating the cream from the skim milk. Cream was delivered down one chute into its own receptacle while the skim milk was carried away into another. She and her brothers made their own entertainment, constructing small pretend trucks out of flat pieces of scrap wood and spending hours riding these around the yard. She attended the local schools and left before she was fifteen to care for her father and brothers while her mother nursed a sick relative. She worked first in Hobart, but returned home after a very short time and then found work locally. She married in 1957, aged nineteen. They had a family of six children. Her husband also fished for scallops and she worked with him splitting the scallops and working in the orchard.

The women in the Huon and Channel in this post-war period went back to a more normal way of life. Modern improvements to technology continued with the telephone now a welcome means of communication. The woman in Case 69 refers frequently to the use of the telephone in their home in the 1950s and 60s. In emergencies a neighbour would be "phoned to arrange transport to the doctor". Even prank calls were a part of her story, causing some distress to the recipients.

Trips to the cinema in the Town Hall at Cygnet were an easy ride in a car. The men of the party would wait in the hotel for the movie to end. Women who had worked with their families in the apple packing sheds took on new rolls. One (Case 6) ran the local Post Office for forty five years, retiring when she was eighty six. She describes the system with the telephone exchange, an exchange which was shared with the Post Office in the next village and connected to the main office in Hobart. "We had two rings by a handle to the exchange....four rings for... and one long and one short for me." (Lowe 1994: 93/94). If the main exchange in Hobart mixed up the rings she could connect to her neighbouring postmistress and they could have a long chat.

Debutante balls were still taking place. The woman in Case 69 found a partner, designed her dress and had it made by a friend. The Ball was a highlight of the year and they practiced a waltz each Sunday night for weeks beforehand. They were presented to the parish priest and the whole occasion was stunning, with the decorated hall full of well-wishers and a sense of camaraderie amongst the girls and boys taking part. She regrets that these occasions no longer are part of the social calendar.

Also popular in the middle years of the twentieth century were beauty "quests" where young women might seek to represent Tasmania in an all-Australian final. (Interview with Madge Lowe, June 2012)

Young woman dressed to take part in a "quest". Photograph used with the permission of Madge Lowe, Margate)

In the 1950s and 1960s the woman in Case 69 describes going with friends to drive-in movies, to sit in the car with a loudspeaker fixed to the car window and a huge screen out at the front.

Others among the women were pursuing careers. Those born in the late 1920s and the 1930s were now grown up. For some it was a time of marriage, for others such as the woman in Case 12, a time to travel further afield, in this case to Sydney, to find work and to expand their horizons. The woman in this instance then returned home and married locally in 1954. Her husband's family had run a local property specialising in hop-growing for many years, with cattle and sheep also raised on the property. The young couple settled in a house across from the hop-fields and the new wife kept up her interests in music, playing with the Middleton Melody Makers .

The woman who returned from war service took up dental nursing and travelled around the Channel having settled to live in the area. She did not marry, but had a number of beloved pets all but one of which perished in the bushfires of 1967 (Lowe undated: 27). Later in life she settled in Conningham, having retired in 1974. The local community recognised the work she had done with an award (Mercury newspaper, January 31, 1989).

Others returned to life on the orchards and farms, some at last able to buy their own land and home (Case 18). In this family the husband supplemented their income by working in the local fish cannery and in the building trade (Lowe 1994: 97/98). Families were still involved in the work of the orchards. Married in 1945, the woman in Case 20 went to work straight away helping to run the orchards (Gardam 1992: 59).

8.2 A childhood in the 1950s

The woman in Case 69 has written extensively of her childhood memories. She grew up as one of a family of seven children on an orchard property near to Cygnet. By the 1950s there still was no running water directly to the house. A water tank with a tap was outside the back door. Water was heated on the fire so that breakfast could be prepared. Morning ablutions were carried out in a basin with cold water from the tank. Bath water was heated on the fire--a once weekly occurrence. The family were the proud possessors of a single tub washing machine with a ringer attached to it. They had a telephone in the house and obviously electricity was connected. The work in the orchards still relied on the muscle power of their horse, but their fruit and apples were transported to town by truck.

The children helped in the chores around the farm, collecting bedding for the pigs and feeding the hens. This woman's particular task was to find the broody hens and to return them to the chook yard. If these hens had chosen to nest in the blackberries rather than amongst the apple leaves in the shed, then the task to evict them was so much harder (Interview, May 2013). With the exception of the connection of "phone and electricity", her description of her childhood might easily have fitted into those two decades previously.

She attended a local Catholic school for most of her schooling and her teachers were mainly nuns. She lists the names of seven nuns. She notes that during this time women, who were lay members of the Church, began to take over teaching duties. The woman in Case 69 left school at 15 having found employment in a local shop and so gaining an exemption from school.

The woman in Case 73 grew up with electricity connected to her home in the Channel. Her father made his wife a present of a washing machine, but she continued to use the copper boiler and at one time Mondays were dedicated to washing. The use of the copper seems to have been an ingrained part of household routine, as with the family of the women in Cases 70 and 71.

8.3 Breaking the mould

The woman in Case 29 was exceptional. By the end of the War she was fifteen. On finishing school in Hobart she returned to the lower Huon and helped her uncle run his orchard. When he died she persuaded her aunt that between them they could carry on the business. She made a success of the venture with her philosophy being "Women can do anything—if they want to be a truck driver, they should be a truck driver". (Hayes. In Hammond 2004: 48)

Having taken over the running of the orchard she became accepted locally for her depth of knowledge about the industry. She was chairperson of the local Apple and Pear Growers group and would address meetings attended by hundreds of men. She maintains this did not trouble her at all. She knew her subject and her subject was apple growing. Her commitment to her work was profound. In addition to her work running the property, her strong religious faith led her to become a lay preacher. At an Apple Festival in 1955 she was crowned Apple Queen. Modestly, she acknowledged that she won the honour through her knowledge of the industry. An interest in the local area led her to set up exhibitions of historical data and she worked to establish a Tourist Information Centre in Huonville. For her service to the community, which included being District Commissioner for the Girl Guides, she was awarded the British Empire Medal in 1983. (Hayes. In Hammond 2004: 50)

8.4 A continuing way of life

The tradition of large families still continued for some. The woman in Case 69 was one of seven children. The woman in Case 72 had five brothers and sisters and her husband was one of ten children. The sisters in Case 74 were part of a family of twelve. The woman in Case 19, having married in 1944, went on to have five sons and three daughters (Lowe. 1994: 100). One woman, already the mother of three children, remarried on the death of her husband. Her second husband brought five children from his first marriage to the union and they subsequently adopted another four children whose mother had died in the 1967 bushfires. Together they raised the twelve children (Lowe undated: 24).

Others with smaller families still managed to help in the apple sheds. When their husbands came home from the war some were able to use re-settlement money from the government to buy property, some bought this property from the family and, with help to mind the children, returned to work to help pay the costs of the enterprise (Watson 1987: 70/71). Local organisations which encouraged women to participate continued to grow. The woman in Case 38 was a founding member of the Sandfly CWA. (Lowe undated: 53/54)

8.5 Fashions change

Just as life-styles were changing gradually for the women of the Huon and Channel in the 1950s and 1960s, so fashions were changing. Dances were still popular and the woman in Case 69 describes her friends starching petticoats on a Saturday in preparation for the night's dancing. In my own younger days they would have been known as can-can petticoats, with layer upon layer of net fabric stiffening out skirts. With these and stiletto heels any young woman would be equipped to steal the show. She also lists the contents of friends' wardrobes —stockings (nylons) with suspender belts, "sloppy joe" jumpers, stove pipe trousers, pedal pusher jeans, dresses called "the shirt that grew" along with the usual assortment of coats, hats and gloves. For a girl of her age these seemed the most up-to-date, modern fashion statements. Add sling-back shoes, make-up, twin sets worn with popper imitation pearl beads (so-called because they clipped together) and the picture is complete. Living in regional southern Tasmania was no barrier by this time to aspiring to the height of teenage fashion. She describes visiting friends who had a record player and listening to the music played at full volume.

Dressed in her finery to go dancing

The Second World War, the Hollywood movie industry, the availability of record players so that the music of American pop stars became popular, increased the influence of the USA among the young and the fashionable. The woman in Case 69 often referred to movie stars and was given a large poster of Elvis Presley as a gift. Even though southern Tasmania was still "at the end of the world", the sense of isolation of the early years diminished as new trends appeared.

Later in the period, (1952) according to Cockerill (1987: 15) townships would hold festivals to celebrate events such as the apple harvest. A highlight of these festivals would be the crowning of a local "Queen". Floats would be decorated, attendants dressed in finery and the Queen would sit, resplendent on her throne, to rule the day's ongoing competitions and attractions. The crowning of a new Queen in England probably encouraged these displays of finery and glamour. For the young women it was another chance to escape from the workaday world, to make and wear glamorous clothes and to parade in front of an admiring community. For the young men there would be a chance to compete in sports, such as wood chopping or to play footy or cricket.

Pearl crown worn by the "Queen" at a Cygnet gala in1910 and again in 1926. Photo courtesy of the Cygnet Living History Museum, 2012.

While the Apple festivals seem to have taken place in the Post World War II years, local celebrations including the crowning of a queen had been in place since 1910 in Cygnet. At Lower Longley a queen was chosen at a gala in 1922 with the gala proceeds going towards a new supper room for the hall. (Lowe undated: 78)

Apple Queen Festival in 1955. Permission to use this photograph was given by the niece of the woman crowned Queen in the picture.

Chapter 9: Natural disasters

9.1 Floods

"Within the space of eight hours the river rose 25 feet above its normal level. Enormous logs were whirled about like corks." (Woolley and Smith 2004: 173)

Fire and flood were (and are) the natural enemies of those settled in the Huon and Channel. In 1854, Woolley and Smith (2004) record that, after a dry spell and fires, the rains came and the Huon flooded disastrously, to the extent of carrying away and destroying boats. In 1858 a further inundation occurred. At Huonville to the present day there is flooding occasionally along the Esplanade and the appropriately named Flood Road still leads into the back of the town.

By the 1950s and 1960s floods were still being recorded. The woman in Case 69 describes listening to Nicholls Rivulet in full flow, with logs crashing into the concrete bridge likened to explosions of gelignite. She would lie awake wondering if their house was safe from the rising waters. In 1960 the woman in Case 45 describes a flood at Longley which washed away a double garage with a car and a motor bike. She adds that a house was washed away at Longley Bridge.

9.2 Early bushfires

"On the rocks and in the water were five women and three children--fire all around them. They were taken aboard the Huon Pine barge—" (Woolley and Smith 2004)

Table 3: Major Bushfires in Southern Tasmania with their associated death toll

Year	Location	Date	Number killed
1854	Port Cygnet	01/01/1854	3
1897	Hobart	31/12/1897	6
1967	Hobart and Region	07/02/1967	62
1987	Southern Tasmania	31/01/1987	nil
1994	Southern Tasmania	04/12/1994	nil
1995	Hobart	01/12/1994	nil
1998	Hobart	01/01/1998	nil
1998	Verona Sands/ Gordon	01/02/1998	nil
2003	Hobart	18/01/03	nil

Taken from "Major Bushfires in Tasmania" (Romsey Australia: http://home.iprimus.com.au)

This table gives a picture of the scale of the 1967 catastrophe in comparison to other bushfire events. It should be noted that the original table does not mention the 1934 bushfires referred to in the early oral histories, so the table above is not comprehensive.

For those working on the land natural disasters could and did occur suddenly, leaving a trail of havoc in their wake. With southern Tasmania naturally covered by forest and with fast flowing rivers from mountain country, it is not surprising that bushfires and floods posed a threat as they still do to this day.

The position of the island, with the hot, dry winds which can blow from the mainland of Australia exacerbates the level of threat. The Huon and Channel districts have a history of bushfire emergencies going back to the earliest days of settlement. The nature of the topography, with forest stretching from the coast to the tops of the Snug Tiers and the hills surrounding the Huon Valley, makes the danger very apparent. As far back as 1853 Woolley and Smith (2004) record a major fire which struck Port Cygnet. Only the bravery of a man serving his time as a convict saved the life of a small child there.

In 1854 in January, the whole countryside was affected by fire. The heat was so ferocious that metal was melted and distorted (http://home.iprimus.com.au). Survivors were rescued by the river steamers such as the "Culloden". These fires extended right up the Channel and at Flowerpot the "Huon Pine" barge took aboard five women and three children who had been standing in the water up to their necks while the fires raged around them. Dwellings were lost at Lymington and at Port Cygnet and as far upstream as Glen Huon and near to Judbury. Again, convict men came to the rescue of those in great danger and again were rewarded for their bravery. Five people, however, died at Petchey's Bay on the Huon and many others were reduced to penury with everything they had destroyed (Woolley & Smith 2004: 172).

Weather conditions in the summer, with drying winds and gales sweeping the area made conflagrations difficult, if not impossible, to control. In the days of bullock carts and horse drawn drays there was none of the modern fire-fighting equipment this generation takes for granted. Even in the present day, with water bombers and fire trucks, the danger of uncontrollable fires remains a cogent threat as has been witnessed sadly in Victoria and in Tasmania in 2013 while this project was being undertaken.

By the early twentieth century, even with the land clearances which had occurred, there were still areas of forest all around the settlements. !934 brought another outbreak of fire, a fire which destroyed the wooden house beyond Judbury which was home to the woman in Case2 (Fenton. In Hammond 2004: 66). This same fire is described by the woman in Case 51, who had been on a day trip by steamer to Hobart. By the time the boat was due to leave for home the sky over Hobart was darkened by smoke. The boat's compass was affected by the fires and visibility was cut by the thick smoke. This led to them going aground on the beach at Blackman's Bay. They had to remain there until the early hours of the following morning when the boat was floated out and they resumed the journey down south (Lowe, undated: 31).

Around Herlihy's jetty on the Huon, houses which were destroyed by fire were rebuilt using wooden palings with the newspaper and scrim covering on the inside (O'Rourke 2008, p.9). In 1938 a bushfire came quickly in the direction of Sandfly. The school was closed and the children sent home. One of the women who was there on that day recalls that she and her brother had to hurry along as the fire was getting close. With only tank water at their home they fought the grass fires around the house with gum boughs. Even her grandmother was out beating at the flames (Lowe 1993: 48).

9.3 February 1967

"My daughter Joyce drove me through the fires on Oyster Cove Road.........The last time I saw my husband he was on his scooter......We tried to get him to come with us in the car but he wouldn't leave his scooter. His body was found at 2.30pm." (Lowe undated: 37)

These events, terrible though they were, are but a foreshadowing of the disaster of 1967. An article found on Trove (http://trove.nla.gov.au) notes that 1361 homes were destroyed on February 7th in the south east corner of Tasmania. The account of a woman who lived through that day states that 653,000 acres of farmland, forest and bush in fourteen municipalities was devastated.

The fires burned to within two kilometres of the centre of Hobart and swept through Taroona on the outskirts of the city. "The Mercury" newspaper reported that the temperature on that day reached 106F, the relative humidity was at 13 per cent and winds topped 73 mph. A reporter, Kay Keavney, for "Women's Weekly" travelled through the devastation with a photographer. Her quote sums up the aftermath. "Everywhere as we drove we saw cars loaded with goods, driven by sad eyed people going heaven knew where. Everywhere we saw families huddled together, picking among the ruins." (http://trove.nla.gov.au).

In her report, according to one of the men who rushed back from Electrona to try to save the town of Snug, the water mains exploded in the heat, leaving helpers powerless to fight the flames. Keavney tells the story of the schoolchildren's survival, a story also told by Gardam (2007), when thirteen teachers, five of whom suffered the loss of home and possessions, guarded the 270 children while Snug burned around the school. According to Keavney, the school buses could not get through to take the children away from danger because a huge tree had fallen and had to be cleared from the road. The safest option was to keep the pupils sheltered in the school. The staff kept the children there until the worst of the danger had passed.

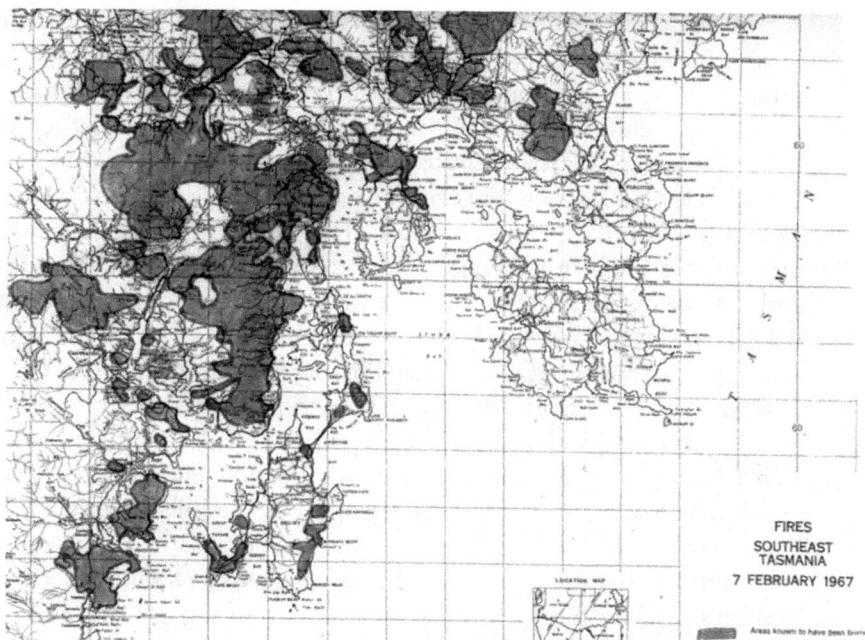

This map shows the areas devastated by the 1967 bushfires. (Courtesy of the Cygnet Living History Museum. 2012)

The buildings at the school which survived the fire became a relief centre, like many which sprang up in the following days. According to Keavney, there was an outpouring of help from all over Tasmania and Australia, to the extent that a shelter was opened to care for stray cats (http://trove.nla.gov.au).

Gardam (2005, 2007) provides a vivid description of events in the Channel on the 7th of February in that year. A small fire had burned at the junction of the Channel Highway and the road down to Oyster Cove. This had been controlled on the 3rd. of the month but logs were still smouldering. On the 7th the temperature had risen and the winds were blowing strongly. The small fire flared and a decision to try to back burn worsened the danger. At about 12.30pm this, now uncontrolled, fire was joined by another coming down from the Snug Tiers. The fire front swept down the Channel with deadly ferocity igniting huge eucalypts like matches and causing houses and outbuildings to explode in flames. There were no fire pumps available.

At Gordon and Middleton the communities were engulfed. (see Appendix 3—Harry Sayer's diary of the day's events). Those living in the area made the best of the bad choices available to them. Some fled down to the sea, some to whatever open ground they could find. One woman tells of lying flat in a potato paddock chewing raw potatoes for moisture and clutching a small pig which was the only livestock they were able to save (Gardam 2005: 170).

In the Huon a land-clearing burn on the Calvert's property at Forest Home near Judbury escaped control. This fire, fanned by the howling wind, missed Glen Huon village and crossed the river at Horseshoe Bend. It swept through Ranelagh killing at least one woman and reached over the Snug Tiers to join the havoc in the Channel (information from the Upper Huon History Group, June 2012). There is less information about the Huon fires in published form. This has been explained to me as being the result of roads being impassable down from Hobart, so that reporters could not gain access. In any case Hobart itself had a major catastrophe in the hills behind the city on that day.

To return to the Channel, Snug lost nine members of the community. Over ninety houses, all the churches, parts of the school and the shops were destroyed completely. The early fire came up from Conningham in mid-morning. Three people died at Conningham, but the fire avoided most of the lower part of Snug. Yet another fire came down from Margate through Longley (Gardam 2007: 160). The woman in Case 12 watched her neighbour's house at Brookfield being consumed by the flames. Her own house somehow remained standing. At Electrona, one street of homes was burnt out.

Later in the morning this second fire, which had come over from Kaoota (the Huon blaze from Judbury?), met up with the fires at Snug. The fire was travelling at such a speed that those in its path had no time to get to their cars. They had to run for their lives holding wet clothes or towels to protect themselves from the flames (Gardam 2007: 163: http://trove.nla.gov.au "Bushfire havoc in Tasmania"). By the time they got to the sea the pine trees around them were burning fiercely.

Seeing the fires coming, women rushed to the school to collect their children. One was asked in addition to take charge of three children whose mother had already died. She made it back to her house, met up with her husband, then collected his parents from their burning house and they all fled to the beach and waded out into the sea (Gardam 2007: 163).

At the school, the children had returned for the first school day of the year. The staff gathered all the children in the school hall and drew the curtains as the Catholic Church across the road was already ablaze. All 270 children were asked to sit on the floor while the music teacher played the piano and led them in song to keep them calm. Then it became obvious that the fire might reach the petrol store at the shop, so the children were moved to the other side of the building. The school tower caught fire and staff rushed to lock the door to contain the outbreak. Throughout this ordeal one staff member noted that "the children were magnificent" (Gardam 2007: 165), but the whole experience left scars in their memories which surfaced each year at the commencement of the summer term. Adults who had come to the school to collect their youngsters stayed to shelter with them. The fire passed, but during the following night the fire in the school tower spread and gutted other buildings (Gardam 2007: 167).

Further down the Channel, the fires which had started at Oyster Cove demolished orchards and farms. Thousands of apples lay wasted on the ground. Some families fought the fires and were able to save property because they had irrigation systems and a water supply. One woman is reported to have saved her home using a mop and a bucket to put out spot fires (Gardam 2005: 170). In the end only three homes were left standing at Oyster Cove and the jetty and shed burned. At Kettering the hall burned down along with St. Mathews Church and the original school at Oyster Cove. Many houses were lost. In one road alone 14 out of the 17 houses burned. A farmer and the local policeman shot 300 badly burned animals. A relief centre was set up at Woodbridge to offer shelter, power, water and food (Gardam 2007: 170).

At Middleton and Gordon in the far south of the Channel the fires left the communities devastated. Homes, churches and schools were destroyed. In Gordon an elderly couple died trying to get to the shore and then to the safety of the sea. The seaweed on the shoreline burned. Those who managed to wade out into the Channel could only watch while their homes were destroyed. The church and the old school, which was also used as a courthouse, were destroyed along with the teacher's house. At Middleton residents were sent to safety in the sea, wading well out into the water. Pregnant women and children were loaded into dinghies and rowed out to relative safety. The main jetty burned out completely. The shop and the Post office building were charred ruins. Some families to the north found shelter in an irrigated paddock (Gardam undated: 99).

There were many families who were forced to leave the area after the fires added to a decline in local industries. There was no longer employment in the area. At Gordon, when Gardam (undated: 101) was writing her history of the area, the community had collapsed. There was no longer a hall, no church, no school, no gaol and no shop. What in the early twentieth century had been a thriving port and apple growing area now boasts few houses. Only a Bed and Breakfast establishment, in 2012, reminds travellers of the name Three Hut Point.

According to Gardam (undated: 88) the community at Gordon in the late years of the nineteenth century and the early years of the twentieth century still boasted a school and a post office. In 1932 a church building was erected which would have stood on the land near to where this photograph was taken as would the hall for the community (Gardam undated: 91).

Looking at the empty landscape now it is hard to envisage a scene described in "The Mercury" (16th. November, 1925). This paints the picture of a ball being held in the Gordon Hall, with refreshments set out under a large tarpaulin in the open air--on a beautiful evening. The space was decorated by the ladies of the community, using silver vases lent by one of them, displays of flowers grown locally and the whole bathed in the glow of a "Gloria Light" again lent for the occasion. The programme included balloon, confetti, streamer and chocolate waltzes, the lucky spot and jazz caps (whatever these were). Pianists provided the music.

Gordon today is almost empty of houses. Photograph by the researcher 29/06/12)

The woman in Case 73 spent most of her life in the area. She was born in 1938. She describes the Gordon of her childhood as having two shops, a post office, a church, a hall, a school (the school house is still there, though the school was burned with most of the other amenities in the 1967 fires).

At one time twenty to thirty scallop boats would be moored round the bay at the oval. There were ten scallop sheds around the bay. The jetty was much larger with extensions at either side. It was a close-knit community where everyone helped and shared---extra catches of fish would be handed out to neighbours, as would spare vegetables. Now there are only a few houses and empty stretches of grass which are sometimes used as camping grounds in the summer.

There is still a jetty at Gordon, but neither steamers nor barges sail the Channel now. The scallop boats have gone. The boat ramp is used to launch small pleasure boats. Bruny Island lies across the water. On the day of the February bushfires the woman in Case 73 describes fireballs being blown from Bruny across this stretch of sea. (photo by the researcher 29/06/12)

Stories of loss and survival on that day are told by several more of the women in this study. For the woman in Case15 the day was traumatic. The family lived near to the shore at Snug. Her daughter was in school. Her husband had just finished a nightshift at the Carbide works at Electrona and was asleep. She wakened him, seized family documents and they raced out to the car. By the time they got started, fireballs were dropping around them. They took neighbours down to the beach for safety. This took several trips.

Her husband then set off to reach the school, on his way picking up a woman with two infants trying to find safety. The car engine was overheating. Seals around the windows were starting to burn and they put these fires out using juice from the children's bottles. He, the woman and the children sheltered in the school for hours. The husband and his wife finally returned to their home after the fire front had passed, to see the final collapse of the walls of the house they had worked on for so many years. They were left with ash and ruin and the clothes they were wearing. Eventually they were able to rebuild their home (Lowe 1994: 51).

In yet another case (Case 52) one woman at Oyster Cove lost her husband in the blaze. He had been confident that the fires were heading away from the district, but then the wind changed suddenly and created what she described as a "holocaust" (Lowe undated: 37). Her husband was very proud of his motor scooter and refused to leave it behind to escape.

Middleton as the fires swept through

At Kettering the men had gone to fight the fires at Oyster Cove earlier in the day. One of the women (Case 54) saw the fire come over the hills behind her property driven by howling winds and with the temperature at 100 degrees. The result was what she describes as "an inferno" (Lowe undated: 51/52). The house escaped the fire but everyone was prepared to go and get into the dam. Damage around was colossal.

The woman in Case 73 gives a vivid description of the day as she experienced it. Her youngest child was celebrating her second birthday at their home near to Gordon. Both her father and husband were away from home.

It was the family custom that her mother, who lived nearby, baked a birthday cake for a family party. Because the day was so hot, she and her mother agreed that a sponge cake bought at the shop would substitute if it was iced at home. The woman set off with the pusher and her two little girls into a howling wind. She bought the sponge cake and took it to her mother's house, then went home. Shortly afterwards the fires came. Fortunately her husband had just finished ploughing around the house so there was nothing there to burn, but fireballs were being blown across the Channel from Bruny Island.

Panel on the Middleton Bushfire Memorial. This memorial was put in place in 2007 to mark the fortieth anniversary of the bushfires. It provides a small garden with seating facing the memorial and features the depiction of a family gazing on all that remains of their home.

The woman had a small pond on the property, which was fed by spring water (she had dug it out for her duck). She and the two little girls sheltered in this tiny pond. She says the smoke was so thick that "you could not see the hand in front of your face". Her mother's house nearby was lost, as was the birthday cake, but her mother's washing still hung on the line, albeit grey with ash. The older woman came and found shelter with her daughter. The older children were at school in Woodbridge and had to spend the night there with friends as there was no way to get them home. After the fires the community was decimated. There was nothing left to allow them to make a living and many had to move. The whole place became very quiet. She also recounts that in the period following the fires there was no electricity in their neighbourhood for three months. Life returned to the patterns of earlier times, with cooking done on the fire, lighting provided by kerosene lanterns and washing done by hand. The old skills were still well known so they managed quite well.

Middleton Bushfire memorial (29/06/12). In the background is the water of the Channel looking across to Bruny Island. The families of the township fled down to there to escape the flames. Young mothers and old women were sent out in the boats while the others stood in the sea and watched the township burn.

119

Newspaper photograph taken in 1967 showing the aftermath of the fires in Snug. The sad remnants of brick chimneys rise skywards in the ashes of the homes they once served. The town is a wasteland. (Courtesy of Cygnet Living History Museum files)

A photograph of the bushfire memorial at Snug taken in 2012 by the author. The memorial takes the form of a house.

Another view of the bushfire memorial at Snug (photo by the author).

9.4 Aftermath of the fires

After the fires in Snug, practical help arrived quickly. By the next day the remaining school buildings housed emergency centres, with the domestic science rooms operating as a kitchen. Clothes and toys and household equipment were donated. An emergency camp for fire victims was established on Snug Oval within two weeks with amenities blocks, huts, vans, lighting and essential services. Even an open air barbecue was on site. A hall was built as a multifunctional centre for worship, pre-school and other amenities. The town's two shopkeepers who had lost their stores operated a small shop near the camp. (Gardam 2007: 168)

Around 160 people were housed in the huts and caravans on the oval. The woman in Case 19, along with her husband and six children lived in a tent and caravan there. They had to wait until insurance money to rebuild was available (Gardam 2007: 168). By the time the Park closed almost a year after the fires, most people had moved into new homes (Gardam 2007: 169). According to the woman in Case 63 these homes were utilitarian and the vernacular buildings of earlier years were not replaced. She describes, for example, the local store which at one time was a gracious wooden building "with a beautiful veranda". This has been replaced over the years with a perfectly serviceable, but plain, concrete block structure.

For the families who lost everything, however, the chance to restart their lives under their own roof would have been a blessing. The woman in Case 12 sums up the mental scars left by the fires "The tragic loss has been hard to forget and each summer the fear always arises that an arsonist will set the State aflame again" (Interview July 2012).

In an interview in 2012 with the ex-president of the Garden Island Creek CWA, it was recalled that the CWA for years (the woman speaking had been president in the 1990s) held a Daffodil Fair in Cygnet. This event commemorated the bushfires which had destroyed much of the area around Garden Island Creek and the new hope which sprung from the blackened ground in the following spring, with the appearance of the daffodils flowering bravely in charred garden ruins. These flowers became a symbol of the strength and resilience of the rural communities.

The woman in Case 63, however, comments in an interview in 2012 that when she and her husband moved back into the family home in around the year 2000, the community in the lower Channel was still trying to regroup after 1967. New families had moved in to replace those who had left the area, but the ideas and changes they brought were not always welcome to all. In her view, the decision to hold a ceremony in 2007 to mark the passing of forty years since the fires and to unveil a memorial to that day helped in healing. Many people who had left the area returned for the occasion and could see that the community was rebuilding. Since then there have been other community reunions.

9.5 In the Huon

While literature and reporting of the fires concentrates on the disaster which struck the Channel, less information exists of the losses in the Huon. As far south as Geeveston, according to the woman in Case 60, the same conditions of heat and wind prevailed. She had been over visiting her sister to do washing when a call from her husband at their property alerted her to the approach of fire. She ran home, collecting her oldest son on the way. She and her son filled as many buckets of water as they could collect and put them all around the house. They then covered their heads with wet towels and patrolled the house to put out spot fires. She describes a "ball of fire" coming down the hill. This drove past the house and travelled along a ridge, burning four homes in its path. Amongst those homes was that of her sister. The mother and son filled the orchard sprayer and her son went off to help elsewhere. Despite being asked to hold the children at school, staff allowed the pupils to get on buses and then her children had to walk home through the aftermath of the fires. (Interview 2012)

For the woman in Case71, the school buses arrived at Franklin on that day to take the children home. As they drove down towards Castle Forbes Bay the hills were "ablaze". She arrived home to find that her mother, a widow running her own property, had spent the entire day hosing down the house and sheds. Conditions worsened and the family was ordered to evacuate. Her mother rushed around loading photos and jewellery into the car. The children were told to choose what they could take. The woman in question could only think that she wanted to save her piano, which was not possible. They drove to shelter with friends nearer to Franklin. Their family home escaped the fires but that of her grandparents further up the hill, which was a wooden two storey dwelling, burned to the ground. She thinks that the presence of large pine trees on the property probably accounted for its destruction (Interview 2013).

The woman in Case 72 was also at school in Franklin. The school buses took her to her home at Castle Forbes Bay. She remembers that her family had apple sacks soaking in the pond and they were all using these to beat out spot fires caused by burning embers falling around the property. Their property was saved but it was late in the night before the family went to bed.

Another interview (2013) yielded a first-hand account of that dreadful day for the people of Cygnet. The woman in Case 69 was at school on the first day of her years in High School. By 11am there was so much smoke around the place that it was getting dark. The nuns who were her teachers knew that "things were getting bad" as the wind was terrible and by about 1pm everyone knew that there were many fires burning in the district. Then fire broke out on King's Hill behind the school. A spot fire caught in the grass behind the school because of blown embers which were burning as they fell in the school yard.

The school bell rang and the students were mustered on the basketball court and walked down to the relative safety of the parking area. They then crossed to the Cygnet Town Hall which was serving as a refuge for families fleeing from Lymington and Wattle Grove. The boys from the Lourdes Hill branch of the school came in soon after. Luckily someone managed to extinguish the fire behind the school buildings.

She recounts seeing a white Holden drive through Cygnet while the students were waiting to cross the main street. One man in the back of the ute came from near her home. The other man she could hardly recognise because his face was black with soot. He was badly burned and was being held in her neighbour's arms. She later heard that the injured man and his mate had been trapped in a Hydro truck between Nichols Rivulet and Oyster Cove. His mate had died of his injuries and the injured man took months to recover.

In the Town hall were mothers with little children who had left their homes, one seeing the woodshed and wash house alight and the clothes burning on the clotheslines. She had left her husband to fight the flames and since she could drive she had picked up other families on the way and brought them to safety. Everyone thought her home had been lost but somehow her husband and eldest son had managed to fight the flames back from the house. Many other families around them were not so fortunate. At Garden Island Creek there was devastation too and everyone in the Hall, which was filled to capacity, thought their homes would be lost. An overflow of people had gathered outside the Hall trying to find shelter.

The school buses came and picked up those who could reach home. The woman in question was one of those. Through the night, although the wind had died down, the glow of the fires was still lighting the surrounding hills and everyone was on the alert. She walked up the road to check on a neighbour with a sick husband. They were safe.

Chapter 10: Life in the 1960s and 1970s

10.1 The decline of the apple industry

"We're usually better organised—you have to be to run a house and work outside and, perhaps, work on the farm too—So if women are out there protecting their farms and their families and trying to re-invigorate the rural communities they usually hang on to the death.." (Bowden 2001: 163)

Data from interviews had suggested that the 1967 bushfires, followed by the decline of the apple industry in the 1970s effected major social change in the Huon and the Channel. This data is, of course, supported by reports in newspapers and in the Report on the Bushfires. However, in some areas nearer Hobart population growth had balanced a loss in more rural areas.

In the aftermath of the bushfires, those families in the Huon and Channel whose properties had either been untouched, or had managed to recover, faced new challenges. In the early 1970s the British Parliament took the decision to join the European Common Market. This decision closed the British market to Tasmanian exports of apples and pears. Even before this the market was difficult with changing tastes and fashions in fruit.

For many orchard growers already reeling from the impact of fire these occurrences were the last straw. The Government funded the dismantling of orchards and encouraged the use of land for pasture. Families sold their properties which were sub-divided into hobby farms. The price of land was low. The woman in Case 75 remarks that in the late 1970s land in the Huon was being sold for $10.00 an acre. The sale of an old Morris Minor van for $100.00 allowed 10 acres of land to be purchased at Garden Island Creek.

The woman in Case 69 notes that throughout her schooldays there were few instances of her classmates changing homes. Not until the late 1960s did families start moving away from the district. She says that those who moved were mostly small apple growers who had been struggling for years to make ends meet. Their families might have been on their farms for many years, but the writing was on the wall and they seized the chance to leave.

Apple blossom still beautifies a property in the Channel. This old orchard supplies apples for juice production. Photograph by the author with permission from the property owner.

A way of life almost vanished. In 2012 there were still individual orchards left, for example one private orchard at Glen Huon and one at Ranelagh (information from the Glen Huon History Group). Between Cygnet and Huonville, in the valley of Nichols Rivulet and on the Channel coast some orchards remain and the production of apples for juice and cider has increased, but the main export crop is now cherries.

The woman in Case 72 recounts that her husband diversified his farm from orchard to dairy cattle. Difficulties in that industry caused a further diversification to cherry crops. For the first time in recent years it is reported that no apples were exported from Tasmania in 2012 because of shipping difficulties and the high value of the Australian dollar (ABC local radio 17/09/2012). For the women, whose working life had centred round the orchards and work in the apple sheds, life had changed.

10.2   Career ambitions

Not only have working lives changed, but preparation for these working lives had moved forward. No longer were the children of families seen as a resource to provide labour on family farms. Expectations could be fostered of careers beyond the Valley and the Channel. Expectations and ambitions might be in place but reality could be different. Two of the women interviewed were growing up in the 1960s and had ambitions to serve in the police or to become market gardeners but their families did not encourage these ambitions and the women found work in local towns.

Schooling was by now centralised in area schools. Some of these took children from early primary age until they could leave school at sixteen. If they had found work, they might be given an exemption from school to start that work aged fifteen. The woman in Case 69 was able to do this when she found employment in a local shop.

To obtain an education beyond the age of sixteen, however, students still had to travel to Hobart to attend what are now called colleges or high schools. In 1937 New Town Commercial High School had opened. As the name suggests it prepared students for work in business. In 1940 the school was renamed Ogilvie High School and until 1963 it took both male and female students. In 1963 it became a girls' only school and has remained so to the present. Private schools such as Friends were open in Hobart and some of those took children as boarders, but this was an expensive option as school fees were paid along with boarding costs. One woman (Case 29) boarded at Friends.

10.3   Community change

Communities were changing as well, as services concentrated in the administrative centres. The woman in Case 71 describes Franklin when she was young (she was born in 1956) as a bustling place where everyone could shop for whatever was required. The small town had a butcher's shop, a chemist, an electrical store, a grocery which also had home goods and hardware, a milk bar, a drapery which also sold shoes, a fish and chips shop and bread was delivered twice weekly form the bakery.

Then businesses began to spring up in the administrative centre of Huonville and Franklin declined. This is the opposite effect to that later described to me in towns like Margate which have become dormitory suburbs of Hobart in the more recent years (see Table 5). Again, in Case 69 the woman telling her story describes one of the shops in Cygnet in the 1960s. She worked in this shop and it sold, apparently, just about everything under one roof. There was a showroom with gifts items such as crystal, crockery, cutlery, vases, statues, and children's toys and music boxes. They sold groceries, men's and women's clothing, jewellery, shoes and slippers, bed linen, brooms, watering cans, hoes and shovels.

In more recent years the small town of Cygnet has two supermarkets, two butchers, a bakery, a vegetable shop, a hardware store, a newsagent, three cafes and restaurants, three garages or repair shops, as well as many and varied small gift stores and it still has three hotels plus the R.S.L.Club.

10.4   Newcomers in the 1970s

Not only were the communities changing in a physical sense, but also in the composition of the population. Families from the mainland moved into the Huon and Channel in search for a more simple, sustainable lifestyle away from the urban sprawl of cities such as Melbourne.

Their advent into a social system which had been stable for two or three generations was not always welcome. They bought land which had been in the possession of local families who had to move due to the collapse of the apple industry. They brought ideas about the preservation of environmental values which were at odds with the long-held necessity of wringing a living from the land. Culturally there was, and probably still is, a clash of values and expectations. The woman in Case 75 felt that she and other new arrivals were categorised as "hippy layabouts" when in fact, in her view, they were working hard to build homes and a new life for their families. In this woman's case she says they received most help from "old blokes" who were still working in the bush and saw and understood what they were trying to do. In the town, she says that it was not until she was pregnant that she felt a measure of acceptance.

Chapter 11: The years from 1980 to 2013

11.1 The impact of change

"Nowadays I live alone, but my family are nearby. I love knitting. I have a computer but I don't know how to use it. I don't watch much television, but I do a lot of gardening and work on the property." (Case 73)

In the last years of the twentieth century and in the early years of the twenty first, social and technological change has impacted on the lives of women in the Huon and Channel area. I have used data gathered through personal interviews I have conducted and through answers to written questions to attempt to identify changes. The women I interviewed were all living at that time in the Huon and Channel and had done so for at least several years. There is no suggestion that the interviews and questionnaire answers provide more than a limited snapshot of the lives of women in the Huon and Channel in this period. A much more intensive study would be required to fully explore the social setting. This was beyond the scope of the present work.

When I first set out to look at the years 1980 to 2013 within this study I anticipated that I would find marked and sudden changes. What in fact seems to be the case is that, despite the markers of the 1967 bushfires and the collapse of the apple industry, change in the Huon and Channel was a gradual continuum in the lives of the women I spoke with who had lived for years in the area. Six of the seventeen participants were born within the area of the research. Three of the women were over eighty years of age and only one of these was born in the Huon and Channel. The other two, however, were born in

Tasmania and spent their childhood in areas bordering the Huon and Channel.

11.2   Childhood

Within the group who were interviewed in 2012 or 2013, or who returned answers to written questions, ten of the seventeen women (Case 74 was based on the story of two sisters) were born outside the area of the Huon and Channel. This would correspond to the notion of a changing population demographic following the exodus caused by the bushfires and the collapse of the apple industry. Of the ten women first mentioned five were born in Tasmania, three were born on the mainland of Australia and two were born overseas.

Of those who were born between the late years of the 1930s and in the 1940s (six women aged over 60 to 80+), two were born in the Huon and Channel and four were born elsewhere in Tasmania. Of this latter four, two were born in Hobart because their mothers travelled there to give birth. They then returned in infancy to the Huon and Channel.

There were nine case studies in which the women were aged between 40 to 60 years (born in the 1950s and 1960s). Of these, six (two in Case 74) were born in the Huon and Channel, one was born elsewhere in Tasmania, one on mainland Australia and two were born in the United Kingdom. Two participants were under the age of forty and both were born on mainland Australia.

Childhood for the older women seems to have followed earlier patterns although, for two of these, long periods of illness impacted upon their early years. Data suggests that six of the seventeen women, in an age group from 60 to 80 years old, recollect being expected to help in tasks around the home and property as children. This would accord with expectations of family responsibilities in the earlier years of the study. For the younger group of women, demands upon them were more in line with keeping their rooms tidy and helping out around the house if required or as rostered. The notion of children as additional members of a family workforce on the land had largely gone. The concept of childhood play did not feature strongly in the stories the women in the early years told to oral historians. No doubt the children played when they had time to spare, but this leisure might have been very restricted by family duties or the time taken to walk to and fro to school.

In later years, participants in interviews told of their brothers' games such as sliding on tin sheets down steep grass banks. One woman born in the late 1930s shared in her brothers races around the yard on home-made pretend trucks. They also raced on a sledge downhill, and the woman tells of opting to sit at the rear for safety's sake. Unfortunately the sledge hit a bush and capsized leaving her under both it and her brothers! (Case 73). Another woman (Case 69) tells of long games spent building cubbies in hedges. Yet another tells of her childhood in Melbourne where the quiet street was a universal playground for hopscotch and skipping and where she took her dolls for walks. (Case 75)

One woman (Case 69) suffered from suspected meningitis as a child. Because her illness occurred in the late 1950s she was hospitalised in the Royal Hobart Hospital. Her memories are of the uniformed nursing staff and the ward sisters in their veils. Her father stayed in Hobart to be near her and she says he would have enjoyed this.

11.3   Education

As might be expected from the above figures the three oldest women interviewed all attended small local schools, one in the Channel, one on Bruny Island and one in the far south of the State. One then progressed to further education in Hobart, one worked in the family business before becoming a nurse's aide, leaving school at around fifteen and one did teacher training before joining a religious order and teaching there.

Place of birth data showed that seven of the seventeen participants attended schools outside the area of the Huon and Channel. Schooling for those who were born and raised elsewhere varied. The two older women are mentioned above. The woman born and raised in London went on to study business. Another attended her local school in Queensland before going on to University for two years. Another attended several schools in Northern Tasmania before going on to University and completing her degree. The woman born in Melbourne attended schools there (she remembers working with slates and chalk in prep class). She went on to attend University at a time when a political initiative had allowed for free university places. The second woman born in the UK was educated there. She then completed her education after immigrating to mainland Australia. She attended University in Australia and completed two University degrees. The woman born in Sydney who answered a questionnaire response moved to Tasmania as a child. Her family moved from Tasmania back to the mainland for a time and so she attended schools in Tasmania, NSW and Victoria. She has completed two University degrees.

Of the ten women who were schooled in the Huon and Channel, one proceeded to study in Hobart having won a scholarship to secretarial college. She returned to work in an office in Cygnet. One was educated at home as she recovered from TB, but went on to complete teacher training in Melbourne and to make a career in teaching and pastoral work.

One woman, in the 60 to 80 age group, left school and opted to go to work on the family orchard. She was offered the opportunity to continue her education and would have liked to train as a teacher. This would have meant leaving the Huon. However, she became engaged and her fiancé wanted her to stay near to him so she remained at home.

One woman, again from this older age group, left school early to care for her father and brothers as her mother had gone to look after a sick relative. She then tried working as a shop assistant in Hobart, disliked this and returned to work with her family and in the local Post Office. These latter two women might, most typically, have fitted the pattern which had been set in the earlier years of the twentieth century.

In three Case-studies (four women) the women were schooled in Cygnet. One went to work locally after school, while the other completed her studies at University. In Case 74 the work patterns of the two sisters in this case-study were not reported to me. Another woman attended school in the Huon then went to Hobart to sit the Public Service examinations and to work in the public service. The other woman, educated near Huonville, went from school to take a child care course. In her adult years she has completed a University degree.

Twelve of the seventeen women in this part of the study had continued their education in the post-school years. Six had attended University though one left after two years. Two had more than one University degree. One of those who worked in a shop immediately after school has gone on to build a career in a specialised area of the social services. Four work or worked in the teaching profession.

These figures provide a dramatic contrast to the earlier years of the twentieth century when University or further education for most women would have been an unrealisable dream.

11.4   Entertainment and community life

By the years of the 1990s patterns in entertainment and community activities had changed. The frequent dances in local halls were a thing of the past. Regular movie nights in small communities had been replaced by trips to Hobart to go to the cinema. Television was standard piece of home furniture.

Organisations such as the CWA still had a place in community life, but were less frequented by younger women. Women living in the area told in interviews of the thriving community activities available for the townspeople. Community activities thrive, but take the form of Yoga classes, pre-school activities for mothers and toddlers, community projects, Art exhibitions and classes, music festivals and local theatre shows, local fund raisers such as bush dances and occasional movie nights.

Cygnet, perhaps, enjoys an advantage in that it is relatively far from Hobart and not close to Huonville, so that the magnet-pull of larger centres is not felt to the same degree as in towns such as Franklin or in those further up the Channel.

In the 1970s as described by the women in Cases 68 and 75, the town was only just beginning to see newcomers arrive. They believe that these newcomers were viewed with some suspicion amongst the older inhabitants. Since these days they say that the district is much more socially integrated.

Cygnet has built a reputation for holding festivals and as a yachting and tourist centre by the sea. Traffic congestion had grown to such a degree that a large new car park is (in 2013) under construction.

Taiko Drum. One of many acts performing at the Cygnet Folk Festival in 2012: photograph by the author. Note the changes in fashion and the casual clothing worn by the women.

Cygnet as it was. Mural on the end of the drapery building. Photograph by the author.

Mary Street, Cygnet 2013. Photograph by the author.

A noticeable comment included in the answers given by seven of the seventeen women in this part of the study was that they cultivated vegetable and fruit gardens. Living in a rural area makes this more possible, and the tradition is strong still in the Huon and Channel. Vegetable growing in the home garden is experiencing a renaissance even in cities.

11.5   Marriage and motherhood

In all but two of the seventeen cases in this part of the study the women were either married, had been married or were in a long standing relationship with a partner. The study "A Small Town" (Dempsey 1992) examines a rural community on mainland Australia in the period 1973 to 1990. The male dominant society depicted in 1973 was diminished by 1990. Women, however, by the 1990s were still typified as wives and mothers and this was viewed, in the particular community studied, as a constant in the meaning system of the community. Marriage and motherhood were very much part of the lives of the substantial majority of the women I spoke to as part of this study.

Of these women, all had children. The size of families was smaller than in the past, with two or three children being the norm. One older woman had six children, one had five. The interview data suggested that, for the younger women I spoke to (aged between twenty and sixty), careers outside the home were now, or had been, also part of their lives. For younger working mothers there could be difficulties in reconciling their career obligations with child rearing and school requirements. This was caused by the disconnection between the expectations of the school system and the expectations of employers. Flexible working hours were available in some instances but school hours have remained fixed in a traditional pattern of a 9am start and a day finishing between 3pm and 4pm. In addition, school holidays remain fixed although a four term year is now in place. For a woman working in business these hours and holidays do not correspond with a normal pattern of work. For some women, for example the participants in Cases 63 and 75, being a "stay at home mum" for a number of years was the chosen option. A teaching career could, however, reconcile care of children with working hours.

Another problem mentioned in Cases 75 and 67 relate to the provision of suitable secondary schooling. Most parents have clear ideas as to what sort of school environment they want for their children. To obtain that environment the family in Case 75 moved to a Hobart suburb for the duration of the secondary school years. In Case 67 the family negotiated their schoolchild's entry to a secondary school which lies on their way to work. This meant the child could be delivered to the school gates in the morning and picked up after school. Unless this had been possible to arrange, the child would have faced a long commute by bus to a more local school. Arranging to catch the bus and to reach home would have been very difficult. These are drawbacks associated with living in a rural area in Tasmania.

Buses still transport children to and from local schools. If, however, the family lives some distance from pick-up and drop-off points the child still has to have transport to these points. Some schools now offer before and after-school child care to allow children to be dropped off earlier and picked up at a later hour at the school. These services have to be paid for. For parents working in Hobart or far from their home, work hours required to be flexible to allow for pick-up and delivery of children to school.

The practice remains that local schools in the Huon and Channel area only provide education till the child reaches Year 10 at around sixteen years of age. To advance to Year 11 and 12 the student has to attend college in Hobart, which can mean parent transport or a bus journey of an hour or more in the morning and a return journey at night. The same difficulties in reaching buses prevail here as in earlier secondary schooling. Given that the younger women I spoke to all either had University degrees or had started degrees at one stage, any young woman aspiring to a graduate degree and living in the Huon and Channel would be faced with this journey to attend college before going on to University. Those women I interviewed with University degrees were (with one exception in Case 72) in careers connected with children and learning which allowed more flexibility in meshing work with the responsibilities of motherhood.

Of the women I interviewed, four of the women had worked with their husbands in family agricultural businesses. By 1994 Tasmania's Rural Woman of the Year was a farmer near Launceston, advising the Government on issues affecting rural women and organising agricultural festivals. She notes that agriculture as a career for women in her youth was "not the done thing" nor was it encouraged (Bowden, 1995: 152). Yet there had been pioneers in the Huon such as the woman in Case 29 in the post-WWII years and cases which tell of a widowed mother or a single woman taking over the running of her property.

11.6   Community support

Views among the women in this part of the study in relation to community support were mixed. Younger women in the Cygnet area in particular were enthusiastic about the choices they had in terms of activities. Three spoke glowingly of the friendships they had formed with women like themselves who were newcomers to the area. One woman in the 40 to 60 age range told how isolated she felt at first when the local community was slow to accept newcomers who opted for an alternative lifestyle. The lifestyle sought embraced ideas of a simpler way of living, closeness to nature and a connection to the environment. This lack of acceptance improved when she and other newcomers formed a sporting team and despite some initial misunderstandings made friends. Another woman, slightly older, told of the group who had come together through the local CWA branch and who still kept their friendships alive though the branch itself closed some time ago. The woman in Case 69 was grateful for all the help and support she had from kinsfolk and neighbours when her home-life was hard.

For others, particularly in an older age group, the pre-occupation with working lives for younger women was thought to detract from the role they could play in community activities. Arranging local fund raising activities means committees and meetings and the busy lives of younger women might not allow time for this. One in particular who raised this point also made the observation that, when she lost her husband in tragic circumstances, she was grateful and overcome by the help which immediately came from neighbours and from the local community.

Rebuilding the spirit which had prevailed before the bushfires was difficult in Channel townships. New ideas might not be accepted in some sections of the community. For one participant in the Huon, her family's support for environmental issues had alienated them from a section of their community who held opposing views in support of the forestry industry. For another, living in an area with a scattered population, meant that the sense of community was, to some extent missing.

11.7   Technology in the twenty-first century

Modern life requires a completely new set of skills. For men and women living in the present times, there may be labour saving devices to take some of the toil out of housework and farm work, but other factors, such as travel time reaching work, have intruded to eat up the leisure hours which they might have expected to have gained.

Just as women in the present day might baulk at slaughtering the family pig, so those living in the earlier years of the twentieth century would be completely lost if asked to deal with modern technology. In an age when running water, connected power from the grid and the luxury of owning a motor car or a radio or telephone were considered marvellous, the instant communications of this century would be mind-blowing. Television and record players were the new marvels of the latter years of the twentieth century, then came computing. To possess not just a computer, but a hand held device which is telephone, computer, television receiver and music provider would be beyond imagining. To be able to travel world-wide within forty eight hours or, nearer to home, to fly to Melbourne in an hour (not to mention having the money to do so) would be unbelievable. To hear of events on the other side of the globe as they happen may seem a mixed blessing to us as we strive to protect ourselves and our children from knowledge that is distressing (Case 68), but to wait for months to have the death of a loved one in war confirmed would have carried its own burden. Warnings of impending natural disasters are delivered nowadays, not only by telephone or by radio, but to mobile 'phones and the progress of such disasters can be monitored on computer web-sites. TV sets require a sophisticated knowledge to handle the number of channels now available.

Women in the latter part of the twentieth century and beyond have had to develop whole new skill sets to cope with the pressure of societal demands and with working environments. It was noticeable that most of the older participants in this study had mastered the use of computers and mobile devices. Not only are skills required, but for many at work they require not only skills, but a higher degree of education to make these skills applicable. These skill acquisitions however, from the interview data with women I have spoken to, do not change the basic responsibilities of family life, as a daughter, a wife and a mother in the Huon and Channel. Despite higher educational qualifications and a much wider scope of work opportunities, the home still has to maintained, children reared, taken to school, educated and cared for. Food may be bought at the supermarket but still has to be brought to the table and these tasks are still primarily the responsibility of women.

11.8 Political awareness

It can be shown that, for women, a greater political awareness has surfaced in the area during the latter years of this study. Now, in the first years of the twenty-first century the Premier of Tasmania, who represents the Franklin constituency, is female. The Member of Federal Parliament for the area is female. Women serve on local councils. Protest Groups in environmental issues are headed by females.

In this study it can be shown that six, mainly, younger women among those I have personally interviewed have firm views on political issues. This is not to claim that politics is shown to be a defining influence in women's lives in the later stages of the study. Rather it can be indicated that there has been an increase in levels of political awareness, whether from a community activist perspective lobbying to obtain funds for projects, or from sympathy with a particular political viewpoint.

One older woman was active in support of the timber industry which is facing decline in 2013. In contrast, five younger women were sympathetic to policies which seek to preserve the natural environment, such as those which seek to restrict forestry to areas of plantation timber. One of these women had taken part in civil disobedience activities on the Franklin River. Another's parents had defied attempts to put in a plantation above a creek which supplied water to their home. Yet another voiced support for the concerns of small business and the role of Government in encouraging self-reliance.

11.9   Working lives

As has already been mentioned, 16 of the 17 case- study participants were either pursuing careers or had, at one time been in the workforce outside the family property. In this area the contrast with the early years of the twentieth century is stark. Three women had worked in offices. Four had been or still are teachers. One was a nursing assistant prior to marriage. Three work or have worked in the retail trade. Three are or have been public servants. One studied child care.

In Case 74, where two sisters were spoken with, their career options were not clarified. While the number of these women who were or are pursuing careers in the workforce is striking, what also may be worth noting is the range of careers which they pursue. In the early years of this study it has been noted that nursing, teaching and shop work were considered "suitable" occupations for women at least until marriage. In these more recent cases, careers in these areas still predominate. Work in a business setting or in the public service has come to offer other career opportunities, with at least two of the women in this field having held managerial positions.

The issue of income also arises here. In the very early years poverty, or at least a shortage of discretionary income, was the norm in the case-studies discussed by oral historians. The women who participated in this later phase of the study could be described as comfortably off, by comparison. The days of making knickers from calico bags out of necessity have gone. Obviously, the amount of incoming finances was not a question asked in interviews. Such a question would have raised issues of privacy. Living costs in the early twenty-first century are, however, much higher than in past years and lifestyle expectations have been raised. Families relying on dual incomes are common. So while the women spoken to appear to live in comfortable affluence, in some cases the truth may be that they have had to work to maintain their choice of lifestyle and to provide for retirement.

Chapter 12: Conclusion

12.1 Interview data collection

I introduced this study with a quotation from James (1989), which speaks of the modesty and endurance of rural women. As I sought to conduct the research project, this modesty was manifest. When I started to approach women to ask for their participation in the study in interviews, I met several refusals. The reason given was that they had nothing to tell which could contribute. "I have not done anything special. You wouldn't want to talk to me." While this was factually incorrect I could not persist when their reluctance was obvious. This, to some extent, accounts for the fact that the interview phase of the study produced fewer participants than I had originally hoped for. Those who did take part contributed valuable data.

12.2 Contrasting patterns

When considering the lives of the women who have lived in the Huon and Channel over the last century, contrasts over time are apparent. During the first decades of the century, life for women in the Huon and Channel had followed a set pattern centred in their local community. Their families were mostly engaged in running small farms and orchards. Transport by road was difficult and unreliable but coastal shipping provided a means of sending the fruit to wider markets and of taking the people up to the main city of Hobart. There were a few small settlements; Geeveston, Franklin, Huonville and Cygnet in the Valley and Margate, Snug, Kettering, Woodbridge, Middleton and Gordon on the Channel Coast.

In the early years of the study families of more than six children were common. Seven of the women in the early years of the twentieth century were, themselves, members of families with over ten children.

One woman (Case 56) had fourteen siblings.

For the great majority of the women childhood years were spent as part of a family unit working on the land. If work in the orchard became a priority, then school was abandoned or at least set aside as a secondary call upon their time. Small properties could and did support the large families. Illness occurred and medical help might be hard to reach but, within the networks of their community, they had help offered and this was gratefully received.

Living conditions, especially in the early years were basic. The slab huts, lined with scrim and newspaper, gave way to larger wooden homes. There was still no running water, with water carried from streams and wells. There was no provision for toilets apart from an outdoor hut set far away from the dwelling. Lighting came from carbide lamps and candles. Washing was done outdoors. While electricity began to be connected in the 1920s and 1930s, this was not available immediately to the majority of rural homes. Cooking was done over open fires or stoves. Work in the home, the woman's province, was labour intensive and hard. To the communities' advantage, however, was their rural lifestyle. Where larger towns and cities of this period might have areas of slum dwellings, crowded living conditions and endemic disease and poverty, at least in the countryside fresh air and space around the family were beneficial.

In the very early stories recounted to oral historians the women make little reference to play in childhood. One was out in the berry fields at the age of five caring for younger children (Watson 1987). This child-minding task was mentioned in several cases where older siblings took responsibility for younger members of the family. The death of a mother could lead to a twelve year old girl taking over the running of the home. One family of girls seemed to have made the task of sweeping out the stable a source of fun (Tinning 1947). Circumstances surrounding the survival of the family as a unit reduced the period we would now regard as childhood to an early introduction to the world of labour.

For the girls growing up in the first half of the twentieth century external world events helped to shape their childhood. The early years of the twentieth century had been marked by the First World War, the Great Depression and the Second World War. All these external events had consequences for the Southern Tasmanian communities. From 1914 young men went to war, leaving behind their womenfolk to carry on the work of farms and orchards. Many of the young men did not return and, of those who did, very few were unscathed by what they had lived through.

When the Great Depression struck, poor economic conditions had already been experienced in Tasmania for some years. The 1920s had been hard financially. For the families living on the land there was still a means to provide food. Shipping apple crops was a problem and returns from the sale of all crops were poor when the crops could be sold at all. Many men were forced into other work to support the payments for their land. Some returned to working in the forests, some found work in the major carbide factory at Electrona. The womenfolk stepped in to carry the burden of the farm work, to reshape old clothing into something which would fit a child, to knit garments and to provide meals with the minimum of ingredients.

Following the effects of the Depression, the world again was at war. Once more the young men of the community were called up for armed service, and in this war more of the younger women found roles in support. In the cities they stepped in to operate factory machines, while in the country they drove ambulances and joined the Land Army. Some went overseas on active service as nurses. For the majority of the women in this study, however, war meant a return to running farms and assisting with businesses.

When the Second World War ended, with fewer casualties than had occurred in the 1914-18 conflict, life resumed a more normal tenor for around two decades. Shipping the apple crop still met with difficulties, for example in the Suez conflict in 1956, when shipments were held up by the closure of the canal. In post war Europe ideas of a Common Market were circulating to bind the disparate communities together. Markets in Britain vanished. These problems were already placing stress upon families accustomed to relying upon orchards and berry farms as a mainstay for their income. Then came the destruction of the 1967 bushfires which, in turn, led to community change.

The age for leaving school was generally set at fourteen. Two women left school before this age to take over care of their families. Only a handful of women in the earlier years went on to education after fourteen. To do so would mean boarding away from home in Hobart. As the century progressed, improved roads and the option of bus travel daily to Hobart increased opportunities for further studies.

In the early years of the twentieth century in the Huon Valley and the Channel schools were small and local. The school building could consist of a single classroom and adjoining this might be accommodation for one teacher. Buildings such as the schoolhouse at Garden Island Creek have been converted to comfortable homes, but the layout of the original school is still plain to see. Children would start in school around the age of six or seven and would have completed their school years by fourteen. In some cases family circumstances would force them to leave at an earlier age.

The curriculum would centre round the basic skills of reading and writing, and basic mathematical skills. Occasionally an inspired teacher might attempt to open windows to the wider world (O'Rourke 2008). The classroom might feature a single long table round which the pupils sat. Work would be done with slates rather than notebooks. When paper, pen and ink were used, then inkwells had to filled up and the teacher had to avoid ink spatter on light coloured clothing.

Inspectors would call at the schools to check on teaching methods. Because there was little transport available to the children, a two or three mile walk to school was common--with the return journey in the evening. Many of the women in this part of the study talk with pleasure about their school years, but it was accepted that any thought of continuing education would be impossible. Even if schools teaching to this level had been accessible, there would have been no money in the family to support this scheme.

By the 1930s provision of schooling had changed. Area schools such as the one in Cygnet and Snug had opened. Children could be transported there by bus. The small local schools were closed down. The curriculum broadened to include practical husbandry and home management skills. Meals were cooked for the "bus children". In Hobart, senior schools teaching secretarial skills appeared, but entry to these was beyond the reach of the majority of girls in this study. On leaving school some of the young women obtained work in local shops or Post-Offices, some went into service in neighbouring homes and the majority moved into work on the family property. Only one attended a boarding school in Hobart, returning after WWII to run the family property (Hayes. In Hammond 2004).

The general pattern for women in Part 1 of the study was to leave school and move into the family workforce. When they married, and fifty six out of the fifty nine women did, their lives continued as before as many of their husbands were also orchardists and farmers. Their childhood training of helping in the home and as part of a family workforce equipped them for their changed circumstances.

Many of these women then went on to have large families of their own. Fifteen women had five children or more. Not only were they running homes in difficult circumstances and helping out in orchards, but they were carrying out these tasks through multiple pregnancies. Latterly small maternity hospitals such as Bowmont Hospital in Franklin at least provided an option of care at delivery. To go to Hobart to give birth was a choice to be made, not a precaution which should be taken.

In the middle years of the twentieth century birth control methods began to be available to women. It would seem unlikely, however, that any clinics supporting these innovations were opened in the Huon and Channel. The only certain method of controlling the size of the family was abstinence from sexual activity. For a married woman this might be hardly practical. Religious scruples might forbid such methods in any case. A woman desperate to avoid a further mouth to feed might take the dangerous step of procuring an illegal abortion.

In Part 2, in two cases, childhoods were spent suffering long periods of ill health involving hospitalisation in Hobart. Two women grew up in the United Kingdom, either coming alone or with their families to Australia. One of the participants grew up in northern Tasmania, one in Queensland and two others came from Sydney and suburban Melbourne.

As children, those who grew up locally were still expected to help out on the family property. For the older women who were interviewed these earlier expectations were more common. For those born around the years of the 1950s and 60s in the rural area there was still an expectation that chores around the property would be allocated to them. Those women interviewed, who grew up in urban environments, or who were in a younger age group reported being expected to help around the house with chores. Childhood games were now mentioned. In Melbourne, the street was a playground. Sports for girls, particularly netball, had become popular. A more carefree time was associated with childhood. There were no world wars, though Australia did send troops to Vietnam. The severe poverty of the early days was a thing of the past with more support available in times of need. A degree of relative affluence enabled families to live a more relaxed lifestyle.

Speaking to the women born in the later years of the century during interviews, it was plain that educational aspirations had changed greatly. For the five oldest women in this part of the study, education would have been provided in the 1940s. Two had still attended small local schools because of the geographical location of their homes. The days of slates and chalk would not yet have passed completely.

Table 4: Contrasts between the lives of women born in Part 1 of this study and the lives of women born in Part 2 of this study

The lives of women in Part 1 of this study	The lives of women in Part 2 of this study
7/59 women were born into families of more than 10 children	2/17 women (sisters) were born into a family of ten children or more
1/59 women were born overseas or on mainland Australia	5/17 women were born overseas or on mainland Australia
41 /59 women indicated that they were born on rural properties	8/17 women indicated that they were born on rural properties
Living conditions, especially in the early years of their lives, were basic for all 59 women. No electric power; no running water.	13/17 women had always enjoyed the convenience of electric power in their home.
In childhood 16/59 women were expected to work in the home or on the property	In childhood 3/17 had set tasks in the home or on the property. These were older women in the group interviewed.
Schooldays: 51/59 women left school at age 14 3/59 women left school before the age of 14 3/59 women were home-schooled 1 received very little schooling 1 continued in school after the age of 14	Schooldays: 14/17 were still in school at age 16 3/17 left school before the age of 16 10/17 continued in further education
2/59 women went on to college	6/17 women went on to University
59 women in Part 1 lived through World Wars and the Great Depression	4 women in Part 2 were children during World War II. There have been localised wars since but no

	world-wide conflicts.
29/59 women married farmers or orchard growers	4/17 women married farmers or orchard growers
Of the women who told of having children 15/40 had five children or more	Of the women who told of having children 2/17 had five children or more
6/40 women had more than 8 children	0/17 women had more than 8 children
38/59 women worked on the land on their properties or those of neighbours	2/17 worked on the land
13/59 women worked outside their homes after marriage	11/17 women worked outside their homes after marriage or in adult life

For these women, one had moved on to become a nursing assistant, one had trained as a teacher before entering a teaching order of nuns, one had boarded in Hobart for a time to attend secretarial school, then had been able to travel daily by bus. The member of this group who remained to work on the family property had aspirations to become a teacher, but elected to stay near to her fiancée. The youngest of the group worked for a time in Hobart before returning to the local Post-Office, manning the telephone exchange.

In the still younger cohort of the women interviewed, school had lasted from the age of five or six until their later teens. The age of leaving school had risen to sixteen, but one woman left early to help care for her family. This occurred in the 1950s. Another gained an exemption at the age of fifteen in the 1960s because she had found work. One woman who had suffered a serious illness had to work hard to catch up on her education.

From elementary work in the early years in Primary school, they would have moved through an expanding curriculum in High School and, in Tasmania, some to college in Years 11 and 12. Shorthand and typing (keyboard studies) might be a part of their training. As the century progressed and the twenty-first century arrived, for the younger women the wonder of television might bring new lessons into the classroom. Needlework and knitting were still skills being taught. In 2013, the one participant still employed in teaching will have a classroom equipped with computer technology.

In these latter cases, one of the women entered teaching after her long childhood illness. Another won a scholarship to study at secretarial school in Hobart. Yet another sat examinations to enter the Public Service. The woman born in London trained in business studies.

University courses were common amongst the younger women I interviewed. For six of them it was possible to move on to University. For one woman this was within her means only because at that time University education had been made free of charge by the Government. All but one of these completed at least one degree. Post-year 12 schooling, or at least the completion of Year 12 is now, in 2013, a pre-requisite for many careers. Yet, to obtain schooling after Year 10, girls living in the Huon and Channel in 2013 must still be prepared to travel to Hobart to attend college in Years 11 and 12. While most of the young women interviewed for this study had obtained degrees, their study in four Cases had taken place elsewhere, in mainland Australia. They had not suffered the disincentive of the long hours of travel to complete school and then to undertake further study which would be the lot of those young women living in the southern parts of the Huon and Channel.

I have stressed earlier that the seventeen cases which form this section of the study were self-selected, in that I was introduced to these women and they agreed to be interviewed. It is possible however that, in the area of education, there may be some bias present. My acquaintances in Tasmania who provided the introductions are well educated in general. There is a possibility that the sample is skewed towards women of similar education. This might account for the prevalence of University trained participants. Anecdotal evidence would suggest that there are still a number of young women in the area who have left school at sixteen, having been discouraged from moving into Years 11 and 12 by the difficulties of travel to Hobart. There might be other reasons, financial, educational or cultural which disinclined them to carry on with schooling. I was unable to make contact with any in this group to ask them to take part in the study.

While all but two in the group I interviewed had either been married or in informal partnerships, the pattern of marrying farmers or orchard growers had changed. Four of the seventeen women I spoke with had taken this path.

By the 1960s the contraceptive pill had made an appearance. Women could take charge of their own fertility simply by taking a tablet daily. Obviously, the ability to control pregnancies must influence family size. Women with higher education and career ambitions cannot afford the time to raise ten children. Not only these considerations but the publicity surrounding the ballooning world population would suggest that families limit the number of children they bring into the world. Never-the-less the women in this study who had married still valued motherhood. Careers had not stood in the way of these patterns.

Married life was, however, complicated by expectations that highly educated women could and should have independent careers. The acronym DINKS (double income families with no kids) was in common usage, but for the women in the second part of this study all but two who were unmarried had children. They were juggling or had juggled career aspirations with child rearing. Their husband's career options had broadened also. There were four women who were married to farmers or timber workers. Most of the other husbands or partners were in paid employment or were self-employed (as in the example of the craftsman making musical instruments).

Career choices have broadened for women in the general population. It is no longer a cause for surprise that doctors and surgeons are female. Woman train as engineers, drive huge earth movers on mine sites, serve in the armed forces, are directors of films and dance companies, conduct orchestras. In this study, however, of the women interviewed in the Huon and Channel, careers were those that, more traditionally, would be associated with women's roles in society. Teaching, social work of various kinds, work in shops and offices were predominant. Perhaps the opportunities to explore other career options are not in place in the area, or perhaps having children and trying to combine careers with child raising has limited choice.

Careers in the late twentieth century and into the twenty-first century, have generally meant leaving home each day to work. No longer was it possible for the women in this sample who were working, to programme their day around housework and work on a farm or orchard. They were obliged to conform to the expectations of an employer. This phenomenon was not new. As the apple industry had become more industrialised women were already encountering these problems. "It was a battle really" (Watson 1987: 71). This caused stress in managing to run a home, care for children and carry out work tasks and programmes. Workplaces are gradually becoming more "family friendly" but the road ahead is still fraught with problems. In this day and age it is possible to "work from home" by means of the internet. One woman in the study (Case 75) used this method to manage her husband's instrument making business, selling these creations on-line. This same women, who arrived in Tasmania as part of the inflow of newcomers from the mainland, noted that in their early days here it was quite usual for the women in the family to go out to earn an income while their male counterparts worked to clear a part of their land and build homes. One younger woman interviewed commutes daily from near Oyster Cove to Hobart to her workplace. Another has a twenty minute drive to reach work.

12.3   Similarities between the lives of women in Part 1 of this study and the lives of women in Part 2 of this study

For twenty six women out of the fifty nine early case-studies their birthplace was in the Huon and Channel. One of the group was born overseas. None had moved to Tasmania from the mainland of Australia. Eight out of the seventeen women interviewed in Part 2 were born in the locally. Those born on the mainland of Australia or overseas were predominantly in the younger group of women.

The great majority of women in both parts of this study had married. In Part 2, however, the question of marital status was not included in the questions I asked, to protect privacy. This was because informal partnerships are now common and divorce is nowadays a factor in married relationships. The information about married or partnership status I am using is based upon conversations I had with the women. Two women in Part 2 stated that they had not married. One of these women had spent her adult life within a religious order.

For women in both parts of this study, a common factor was that those who had married or had been in a partnership had children. The numbers of children in the family might have declined sharply but the experience of motherhood was common to both groups. Statistics given in the 2011 census for the Kingborough area indicate that the average family size now equals 1.8 children in each family. In the Huon

Valley the number given is 1.9 children in each family. This is a far cry from the days of having over a dozen siblings, as experienced by women in the early twentieth century.

Table 5: Similarities between the lives of women in Part 1 and the lives of women in Part 2 of this study

The lives of women in Part 1 of this study	The lives of women in Part 2 of this study
26/59 women were born in the Huon or the Channel	8/17 women were born in the Huon or the Channel
3/59 stated that they had not been married	2/17 women stated that they had not been married or in a partnership
40/56 women listed having children in their life stories.	15/17 women had children
8/59 women worked in shops or Post offices 4/59 women were nurses or midwives 1 woman was a teacher	3/17 women worked in shops 4/17 women were teachers 1/17 was a nursing assistant

12.4   Changes to leisure pursuits

In the early years of the twentieth century whatever entertainment was available tended to be centred round the home. Pianos feature in many of the earlier case-studies. Making music was a shared family pastime. As the years passed and travel became easier, then the community became the centre of activities. Balls and evening entertainments became popular. Small community halls were built and events might take place in the open air. Dances became a regular event with those attending travelling long distances, by foot, by horse and dray, by boat across the Huon and in later years by cars and bicycles. The young women of this period made their own clothes and sewed by lantern light to fashion dance dresses.

In this period the showing of films came to the area, in the form of the "Travelling Talkies". Film nights were popular, but the schedule for film showing and dances had to be carefully arranged to ensure that there was not a clash of venues. Radios began to make an appearance in homes (run at first by carbide batteries). Listening to radio serials became a popular way to spend time. Also, of course, news from abroad and mainland Australia could reach the Huon and Channel in minutes rather than in days and weeks.

These leisure pursuits continued into the 1950s and the 1960s. The "Travelling Talkies" ceased after a period of around fifty years, but the movie shows continued in Town Halls and in drive-in cinemas. Record players brought popular music into the home. Soon the wonder of television was a new staple in the world of entertainment. The telephone brought families together.

By 2013 the relatively new concept of computing has introduced society to the world of instant technology. Mobile 'phones are a standard part of daily life. Record players were replaced with CD players and these are now superseded by tiny portable devices capable of holding entire music libraries. Dances as a gathering place have been replaced by city night clubs. DVDs bring movie watching to large home screens. Even the oldest participants in the second part of the study were adept at utilising mobile 'phones and lap top computers (though one confessed she used her computer to play cards rather than to communicate).

There were still locally organised activities. Amateur theatre groups put on shows. Bush dances were held to raise funds. Special movie events might be held in the small towns. These activities were sporadic rather than a regular established part of community programmes. The State capital of Hobart, now within relatively easy reach, drew cinema enthusiasts, concert attendees and provided the major drawcards in cultural and social events. A level of sophistication had come to leisure activities in the Huon and Channel.

Table 6: Leisure pursuits through the years

Early years of the study	Later in the study
Families would gather round the piano to sing.	Dances were still popular
Church services would be held in homes	Movie nights continued: Drive-in movie theatres appeared

Husbands would read aloud to their wives and daughters as the women sewed	Radios came into homes. Record players appeared.
Dances and balls began to be held in community halls	Television came into homes. Video players allowed movies to be watched at home.
Movie nights would be held in halls	Computers brought the internet into homes. CDs replaced record players. DVDs replaced video. Mobile 'phones appeared. Ipads and hand held devices were common.

12.5   Changes within the communities

"In earlier days everyone knew everyone else. All were prepared to help a friend when needed and every township was a close-knit community. Those were good times." (Lowe undated: 28)

As the twentieth century progressed the small communities in the Huon and Channel grew. Society, however, was still close-knit and inter-linked by kinship ties. To survive in a still remote locality this degree of self-help and neighbourhood co-operation was essential. Medical help could be hard to reach and women who were skilled nurses were invaluable. Mothers often had to rely upon time-honoured "cures" passed down through generations. If a family struck trouble or hard times their neighbours would step in to assist wherever they could. The communities came together in sorrow and in celebration. Through local events young men and women met and might subsequently marry. Through wars and hardship the ties of community held firm.

A huge marker in the lives of the women, in the Channel in particular, was the bushfire catastrophe of 1967. When talking to participants in the study who had experienced that day, this fact became starkly clear. Orchards were destroyed along with livestock and property, but most terrifying was the loss of so many lives.

The pattern of life, especially in the Channel was completely disrupted. Small communities such as Flowerpot were devastated and were not rebuilt. Many families moved away and were replaced by newcomers in what had been an area where few changes had taken place over decades. The established pattern of life was dislocated. The intricate web of family and neighbourhood connections was partially severed. When Britain took the decision to join the now established Common Market, the final cords of sustainability for the orchard growers were cut. Government grants allowed for the uprooting of apple trees and many families took the opportunity, either to sell the properties and see them sub-divided into hobby farms, or to turn the land over to pasture for cattle.

Table 7: Changes to Margate in last forty years based on information from Madge Lowe

1970	2012
Small country town	Semi-suburban enclave
Everyone knew everyone else	Population has expanded with housing developments. Many people are now strangers.
Had churches and small stores and a school	Has doctors and physios, a chemist's shop, pizza outlet, video stores, supermarket, hair salons, hardware store as well as churches and a school.
Quiet roads with few cars and trucks	Main traffic artery to Hobart, commuter traffic, heavy goods traffic
Journey to Hobart by the coast road and Taroona	Kingston by-pass has much reduced travel time

There is at present (2013) no direct overseas shipping service from Tasmania. All goods have to go via Melbourne. The only overseas market left for apples is in Taiwan. Those selling apples nowadays have markets on the mainland, where once the market was an off-season crop to Europe. This market has been closed for years. There is still a market in Tasmania for apples to be juiced (Interview with orchardist: 2012) but this may close. A new cider making industry is in its infancy. For women married to farmers, the effects of change have been obvious. As one woman, (Case 72), put it "The only time we made money was the day we sold the farm.".

A new society began to build in the area. On the small five acre lots which became popular, families set out to re-create a dream of a simpler life closer to the land. Land was cheap and, in the 1970s, $10 dollars would buy an acre of land around Cygnet. City life for some had become too crowded and stressful on mainland Australia.

The newcomers were not always welcomed with open arms. Having endured and lost so much, the established society looked askance at "hippies" arriving to make homes on the fringes of the forest. It has taken years for the two diverse streams of community life to integrate to some degree and to feel comfortable with each other. Stresses persist. A desire to protect and conserve the unique environment of Tasmania can conflict with long-established traditions of land use and forestry.

Three of the women interviewed still owned properties on acreage. For one family this is a large area of natural bush. For two others there is pasture and bush with some land more extensively cultivated for gardens and vegetable crops. The remainder live on properties in the small towns and villages or in nearby countryside.

What did not seem to have changed was the degree of satisfaction, at least around the Channel and the Cygnet area, with community support and activities. Women who had recently made their homes in the area had found support amongst other newcomers. By the time of writing, all were at home in their new surroundings and absorbed in local activities. Two of the women who lived in the Upper Huon Valley expressed the opinion that their communities were more scattered nowadays and therefore the provision of community activities was more difficult.

In the early years of this study life had been basic for families. Although living conditions had improved with more settled communities, any work in the home or on the property was labour intensive and time consuming. The simple task of washing clothes took on labour of mammoth proportions if a woman was washing for herself, her husband and a family of six or more children. Most modern women would give up the task. Multiply this labour by cooking for and feeding a large family, then add responsibilities in the orchard and packing sheds, milking cows, making butter and cream, sewing and mending and it will come as no surprise that women of that era had little time for anything other than daily activities.

12.6   Changes to technologies

Table 8: Contrasts

In the early years	The later years of the study
Basic tools: Horse drawn transport	Cars , trucks, buses
Washing tubs, mangles, copper boilers	Washing machines, tumble driers
Cooking on open fires	Electric cookers, microwave ovens
Newspapers for news	Radio, television, computers with Internet
Brushes and shovels for cleaning	Vacuum cleaners, electric polishers

Then came the advent of electricity and, wonder of wonders, a machine which would do washing. True, for many this was an unaffordable mirage for years. The promise of a less arduous future was in sight. Candles and lamps were supplanted by electric light in the home. Basic refrigerators came onto the market. Radios could be purchased. Life was becoming easier. Motor cars replaced the horse and dray. Buses began to run on routes to Hobart.

Women learned to drive. Among the women I interviewed one who has retired drives to do voluntary work in the Hobart city. One drives to Hobart each day to work.

One of the oldest participants recently gave up her driving licence, very reluctantly, and uses an electric chair to access the shops. The use of cars, technology, and household appliances is taken for granted. Scarce public transport in rural areas makes car ownership mandatory. Nine of the participants are retired from work but seven are still fit enough still to run their homes and gardens unaided. All drive or have driven cars.

In the twenty-first century these improvements are taken for granted. Not only do homes have a vacuum cleaner to replace brushes and mops, but now robotic cleaners are advertised which will do the work unaided. Washing machines operate on a set program which presents the finished and spun laundry. The only effort is to choose whether to hang this out to dry or to use the tumble drier.

Main Street in Huonville: 2013

Not only do families take television for granted but they expect to possess mobile 'phones, internet on demand and all the other wonders that computer technology has introduced. Life has been made much less labour intensive but work and careers have moved in to fill what seemed like promised leisure time.

12.7　Changed political interests

Despite women being given the right to vote in the early years of the twentieth century, there was little evidence of political interest in the accounts of their lives in the earlier years of the study. The concept of women's liberation does not seem to have made a great impact in this remote rural area. To some extent the notion of liberation would have been foreign to them. They were already working side-by- side with their families or husbands on the land. The husband took out loans in his name, but the whole family's livelihood depended on these loans being repaid, so the women were partners in this enterprise. They would undertake tasks usually regarded as the province of the man in the family when necessity forced them to do so. There was no suggestion of a life of leisure and perhaps boredom, associated with wealthier women in more urban settings. A rudimentary education does not foster confidence to speak in public.

Among the women whose stories are told in the second part of this study there was evidence of more marked political interests. This did not mean that adherence to any given political party was stated. Rather a more general interest in particular causes was expressed.

One of the older women had a life-long connection with timber communities and was upset at changes which are taking place in that industry. She was actively involved in supporting the continuation of forestry. For five other younger women, the protection of the natural environment was said to be of importance in their lives. Two had taken part in protest marches or campaigns against proposals to alter this natural environment. One remembered her parents campaigning against a proposal to plant plantation timber above a creek which provided them with water. This same woman endorsed the teaching union, of which she is a member. Yet another woman viewed politics from the perspective of a small business owner, arguing that members of society should take responsibility for their own lives and not constantly look for outside help. In one case, the woman was prominent in community work and negotiated with local and State politicians for project grants.

Table 9: Timeline for the political enfranchisement of women in Tasmania

1902: The Commonwealth Franchise Act: Women who were British subjects, over 21 years of age were entitled to vote for Federal Parliament and to stand for parliament.
1903: Women became eligible to vote for members of the House of Assembly. Franchise to vote for members of the Legislative Council was limited to owners of freehold property to the value of ten pounds or leasehold property to the value of thirty pounds. This was extended to women.
1911: Compulsory enrolment to vote.
1913: Alicia O'Shea Patterson became the first woman to stand for election to the Commonwealth Parliament from Tasmania.
1920: Women who had served as nurses in WWI were eligible to vote in Legislative Council elections.
1921: Women became eligible to stand for election in the Tasmanian House of Assembly.

1941: Franchise for the Legislative Council was extended to all servicemen and women in any war. The age limit was reduced from 30 to 21.
1943: Dame Edith Lyons from Tasmania was elected to the Federal House of Representatives.
1948: Margaret McIntyre was the first woman to be elected to the Legislative Council in Tasmania.
1954: Spouses of property owners became eligible to vote in Legislative Council elections.
1968: Full adult franchise (over 21 years of age) for the Legislative Council.
1973: Voting age for Federal elections reduced to 18 years of age.

More recently Lara Giddings has become Premier of Tasmania. Julia Gillard has been Prime Minister of Australia. The current Federal MP for the constituency of Franklin is a woman. The Governor General of Australia is female.

12.8   Summary of the study findings

Changes over the period 1900 to 2013 in childhood patterns and the expectations of families are obvious. No longer are children seen simply as a useful adjunct to the family workforce.

Leisure had been a scarce concept in the early years of the study. Not until roads improved did the community take centre stage. The families joined together in fund-raising events such as balls and movie shows. In the modern life of the Huon and Channel community activities are many and varied with festivals, education classes and special events. Tourists are drawn to the beauty of the Huon and Channel and to fairs and folk festivals.

What has not changed in the lives of the women in this study is the pattern of daily work in homes. In the early years the effort taken to feed, clothe and provide for a family which could number ten children was immense. In general, family sizes have decreased markedly. Changes to the ability of women to take charge of their own fertility must have impacted upon birth rates especially late in the twentieth century and into the twenty first century. The large families of the early years have all but disappeared. In the latter part of the study only one family had six children. The mother of these children was in her seventies when I spoke with her. For most of the mothers the number of children was two or three.

Later interviews showed that, while families were much smaller, this work was now complicated by career aspirations. The basic assumption of a woman's responsibilities for home-making and child-rearing did not seem to have changed. Certainly there is anecdotal evidence of a more equal gender-sharing of roles now that women are entering the paid workforce but, in this study, the women still regarded themselves as primary care-givers and home-makers. In entering into marriage they all accepted these roles. The majority were or had been married. For some of the women in the later years there have been changes, in that marriages have ended in separation or divorce and new partnerships have been formed. While the aspect of their lives concerning relationships was not directly enquired into, in conversation these facts became clear.

Community life was impacted by wars and the Depression but the greatest effect was caused by the 1967 bush fire disaster, especially in the Channel. Community infrastructure was destroyed. This and the subsequent collapse of the apple industry have brought demographic change. Properties were sold and newcomers moved into what had been a very stable population. Like most change this brought about friction. This friction has lessened over the years but points of difference still arise particularly over land use and the protection of the environment. The responses to questions directed towards political interest demonstrated this fact.

That the years of the twentieth century were marked by huge changes world-wide is indisputable. These changes have accelerated as society moved to a new millennium. Even in such a remote part of a remote island, such as Tasmania, the acceleration of change is evident. For the greater part of the twentieth century life continued in a settled pattern for the women and their families despite world events. Then sudden change came with bushfires and the apple pull and disrupted these patterns. The community is still rebuilding.

The rural setting of the study area is significant. As Young (2008) noted in "Abernyte", that small rural parish was being impacted upon more and more by the growth of the city of Dundee in Scotland in its near vicinity. In the Huon and Channel, more and more functions of business and Government are centralised in Hobart. What were small, intimate, local communities have expanded into semi-suburbs. These experiences in rural communities must be reflected world-wide as city living becomes predominant. At the same time, rural industries which supported the population may be under threat or have suffered severe decline, such as the orchard industry as depicted in the research, or in the present time, the local timber industry. Readjustment can be a painful process and social fractures can appear. The smaller the community boundaries the more hurtful and damaging those fractures can be.

In world-wide historical terms a period of just over one hundred years is a fleeting moment. For European settlement in southern Tasmania it represents a major portion of that aspect of the island's history. With no written records of the long standing human occupation which was in place prior to convicts and settlers arriving from the northern hemisphere, the period of the twentieth and early twenty first century forms the mainstay of our knowledge of history in Tasmania. It has seemed important to me to explore and analyse the social settings of these years, using the oral testimony of the women who have lived here in the far south. From this analysis, I hope we may learn lessons from the past of the perseverance and struggle which have allowed the community of the Huon and Channel to form, to prosper, to meet change and to adapt.

References and Appendices

References and Appendices

References

Alexander, A 1991, The Public role of Women in Tasmania: 1803-1914, PhD. Thesis in the School of History, University of Tasmania, unpublished.

Beresford, Q 1983 The World War One Soldier Settlement Scheme in Tasmania, Tasmanian Historical Research Association, Volume Thirty No. 3.

Beresford, Q. 1982 That Dreaded Plague: Tasmania and the 1919 Influenza Epidemic, Tasmanian Historical Research Association, Volume 29, No. 3.

Borchardt, D.H. 1960 Checklist of Royal Commissions, Select Committees of Parliament and Boards of Enquiry, The Wentworth Press, Sydney, Australia.

Bowden, R 1995 Women on the Land: Stories of Australia's Rural Women. ABC Books, the Australian Broadcasting Corporation, Australia.

Burton, D (ed.) 1957 A Short History of the Huon, Huon Tourism Council, Tasmania.

"Centenary of the Settlement of the Huon", Huon Newspaper Co. Pty. Ltd., Franklin, Thursday 17th. December 1936.

Cockerill, J 1987 "A Brief History of Cygnet", self-published.

Country Women's Association in Tasmania, 1996 Playing Our Part. Sixty Years of the Country Women's Association in Tasmania, CWA, Tasmania.

Dempsey, K 1992 A Man's Town. Inequality between Women and Men in Rural Australia, Oxford University Press.

Friend, R 1992 We who are not here, Huon Municipal Association and South Eastern Aboriginal Corporation, Tasmania.

Gardam, J undated Three Hut Point: a history of Gordon and Middleton, self-published.

Gardam, J 1992 Peppermint Bay: a history of the Woodbridge area, self-published.

Gardam, J 2005 The Oyster Coves: a history of the Kettering- Oyster Cove area, self-published.

Gardam, J 2007 The Snug: a history of Snug, Electrona and Conningham area, self-published.

Garnsey, A 1944 Romance of the Huon River, Whitcombe and Tombs Pty. Ltd.

Hammond, D (ed.) 2004 Heroes of the Huon, Huon Eldercare Foundation, Tasmania.

Henning, P 2006 First World War, Centre for Tasmanian Historical Studies, www.utas.edu.au/library/companion

James, K 1989 Women in Rural Australia, University of Queensland Press.

Kelly, P 2001 The Australian Story, Allen and Unwin, Australia.

Lowe, M undated "Days Gone By in the Channel, Volume 1" self-published.

Lowe, M undated "Days Gone By in the Channel, Volume 2" self-published.

Lowe, M 1993 "Days Gone By: Sandfly, Kaoota, Pelverata and Lower Longley", self-published.

Lowe, M 1994 "Days gone By in the Channel, Volume 3" self-published.

Lowe, M 1998 "I Pass This Way But Once", self-published.

Lowenstein, W 1978 Weevils in the Flour, Hyland House.

Mc Calman, J 1993 Struggletown: Richmond 1900-1965, Melbourne

University Press. Australia.

McLeod, R 2005 Thrift and Fantasy: Home Textile crafts of the 1930s—1950s, Harper Collins, New Zealand.

O'Rourke, T 2008 Recollections of a Centenarian, self- published.

O'Malley, L 2009 Clever ducks, self-published.

Perrin, R.A. and Hay, P.R. 1987 Tasmanian Scallop Industry: Problems of Management, Papers and Recordings of the Royal Society of Tasmania. Volume 121.

Roe, M 1999 Life over death: Tasmanians and tuberculosis, Tasmanian Historical Research Association, Hobart, Tasmania.

Scott, J 1986 Girls with Grit: Memories of the Australian Women's Land Army, Allen and Unwin Pty. Ltd., Australia.

Tinning, R.E. 1977 Backward Glances , self-published.

Townsley, W.A. 1991 Tasmania from Colony to Statehood: 1803-1945, St. David's Park Publishing, Tasmania.

Watson, C 1987 Full and Plenty: An Oral history of Apple growing in the Huon Valley, Twelvetrees Publishing Company. Australia.

Woolley, R 2002 ' Above the Falls. The People and the History of the Upper Huon, self-published.

Woolley, R and Smith, W 2004 A History of the Huon and the Far South. Vol. 1 Before the Orchards Grew, Huon Valley Council, Tasmania, 2004.

Young, M 2008 Abernyte. The Quiet Revolution, Perth and Kinross Libraries and Lifelong Learning, Scotland.

Appendix 1: Case Study participant information

Introduction

This lists in the first instance the location of the early case-studies in the literature. There then follows a summary of the case-study participants who were interviewed or answered written questions.

The first 59 Case Studies are taken from the work of earlier historians. The list below identifies the sources of these Case Studies.

Cases 1, 2, (Hammond (Ed.) 2004): Case 3 (Garnsey 1944): Case 4 (O'Rourke 2008): Cases 5, 6, 7, 8, 9, 10, (Lowe 1993): Case 11 (Lowe 1994): Case 12 (Lowe 1998): Cases 13, 14, 15,16, 17, 18, 19, (Lowe 1994) : Case 20 (Gardam 1992): Cases 21, 22, 23, 24, 25, (Gardam 2007): Cases 26, 27, 28, (Watson 1987): Case 29 (Hammond (Ed.) 2004): Cases 30, 31, 32, (Watson 1987): Cases 33, 34 (Woolley 2002): Case 35, (O'Malley 2009): Cases 36, 37, 38, 39, 40, 41, (Lowe 1993): Case 42 (Tinning 1977): Cases 43, 44, 45, (Lowe 1993): Cases 46, 47, 48, 49, 50, 51, 52, 53, 54, 55, (Lowe undated): Case 56 (Cygnet Living History Museum, Folder 10): Case 57 (Cygnet Living History Museum, Folder 8): Case 58 (Watson 1987): Case 59 (Cygnet Living History museum, Folder 1, CLH 00218)

One woman (Case 12), whose story is told in earlier histories and in an autobiography, also was interviewed by me in connection with the study. I have included her details here and below because of our conversation.

Additions to Case study 12, added after interview

The woman in Case Study 12 wrote the four volumes of local history about families in the Channel and also her own autobiography. I got in touch with her to seek permission to draw upon her earlier work. She was kind enough to see me twice and has expanded on the information provided by earlier works.

She, at the time I spoke with her, lived in the house she grew up in as a child and she showed me around the house explaining the changes she and her husband have made. The old apple shed still stands in the back garden and is now used as a workshop by her husband. The land which once was given over to orchards now houses thirty five new homes. The paddock below the house, which was pasture for the family cow, now is taken over by a new restaurant.

Her brothers used to wear the seats out of their trousers sliding down the slope to the paddock on pieces of tin. She also provided me with photographs which I have permission to use. She was, at the time of interview, still active in the community, playing piano for a local singing group. She was a member of a local dance band for many years playing at dances in the Channel area.

Case study: 60

The woman in case Study 60 was born in Queenstown around 1930 and moved when she was very young to near Recherché Bay in the far South of the island. Her father was a saw miller. She was one of nine children, having four brothers and four sisters. She went to school at Leprena. They walked three/four miles roughly to school. From their house they could see the SS. James Craig anchored across the bay. The saw mills at Leprena closed and her father moved his operation to Cockle Creek. He offered to build a school for the children at Cockle Creek but World War II intervened and the building was sold.

The woman then did her schooling by correspondence but felt she wasn't learning anything much. By this time she was helping out at the saw mill and was tired in the evenings anyway so she stopped lessons. She would have been fifteen or sixteen. She was bundling lathes at the saw mill, a hundred lathes to the bundle. The war had meant that her father's workforce had left so the children stepped in to keep the business going. The woman was a "left handed tree feller" climbing up onto a felling platform to take the trees down. Her sister learned to fire the steam boiler, under her father's supervision, which drove the engine to haul the logs to the tramway to be taken to the mill.

Another sister kept the accounts for the business. Her uncle was the captain of the three masted schooner the "Alma Doepel", based in Melbourne, which was one of the ships which came to collect timber. On bonfire nights he would contribute spare ship's rockets to the festivities.

Eventually her brothers and sisters left home but she stayed to help her mother with the shop she was running at Cockle Creek. At the time her father was building a fishing boat. When the boat was finished the woman came to Franklin to help a local woman look after her children while she was pregnant. While she was doing this she met the local doctor who suggested she would enjoy nursing so she then went to the Bowmont Hospital in Franklin as a nurse's aide in the labour ward there. She shared a room upstairs in the building with another young woman from Franklin.

She had met her husband at dances at Lune River and Hastings and met him again at dances in Franklin. They were married in 1950. His father had an orchard at Geeveston and gave the young couple land to build a house. They lived in Geeveston for sixty years and had six children. The woman worked in the packing shed. The orchards were left to her husband's younger brother who eventually became tired of the work. The woman and her husband took over the farm and farmed cattle. Then her sons bought it. She used to help them around the farm. She drove a one ton truck loaded with hay bales. The cows would run down the paddock when they heard her calling.

The woman has travelled around Tasmania. She had hoped to visit Port Davey on a cruise ship from Hobart but rough seas prevented the ship going along the south coast. Her reason was to visit the area where her paternal grandfather and grandmother worked as Huon Pine loggers. She has also travelled up the east coast by boat.

In addition to her farm work she volunteered as a driver to take elderly people from her small community to doctor's appointments. Her car wore out and she started fund-raising to buy a community car for the purpose. The then Premier of Tasmania heard about the effort and arranged for a grant. Twelve people then became volunteers to share the driving.

Her husband became ill and had both legs amputated. At first she "just did what needed to be done in terms of caring for him", but eventually she could not cope with his care and he entered Huon Eldercare nursing home where he died. His widow moved to

Huonville where she now lives. Her health gives her some problems but her spirit is indomitable still. She uses her electric wheelchair now that she can no longer drive her car. She spins, knits and sews as a contribution to local charities. She uses her computer and keeps in contact with family and friends by her mobile 'phone. She helps support the cause of the local timber industry.

Case study: 61

The woman in Case 61 was born at Moogara near New Norfolk around 1924. I originally went to see her to look into the history of the Josephite Convent in Cygnet. She believes that the "Old Schoolhouse Tearoom" in Cygnet was the original schoolroom where the nuns provided education and that what is in 2013 the chemist's shop may have been the original convent. The present convent building was built around 1907. There are now three elderly nuns left in the convent.

Both her parents were born in Cygnet and she taught at Woodbridge and Cygnet. Her mother and father moved to Bruny Island, where she grew up on the other side of the D'Entrecasteaux Channel. She attended summer schools run by the nuns in Cygnet (the priest at Cygnet was responsible for the parish on Bruny) and decided at an early age that she would join the religious order, despite her father's strong objections. Her father was originally a saw miller, but in a fight in which he was set upon by several men he damaged an arm and subsequently had to have the arm amputated. When the family moved to Bruny he worked as a builder. The woman was the oldest of seven children.

When she was three she contracted polio. In spite of her violent, toddler objections and struggles (she laughs about these and says she must have learned some of the words from her father's mates) she was admitted to hospital in Hobart and then later sent home to Bruny where she was confined for two years to bed strapped into a splint which stretched from her waist to her feet. Even when, later, she was allowed to spend time out of the splint she was placed back in this overnight. The illness left her with one leg which was lame. Despite this, when she was able to start school at around the age of eight, she walked three miles each day to reach school. She remembers with gratitude a local boy who had a bike and would allow her to ride pillion down the hill to her home at the end of the day. She wanted to go to high school but, while her sister passed the exam, she failed. Around this time she went to the summer schools in Cygnet and decided that she had a religious vocation. Eventually she was accepted to attend a school in Launceston and then trained as a teacher. She returned south and taught at Woodbridge while her father tried to change her resolution to become a nun. After eighteen months she resigned from teaching and joined the convent. She returned to teaching in the final year of her novitiate and worked in schools all over Tasmania.

When she retired from teaching she looked after members of the order who required nursing. She was able to bring her elderly mother there to care for her. She then undertook parish work wherever she was needed before returning to Cygnet two years ago to live in the convent there. At the time of interview she was still active in the community, still drove and was part of the Cygnet Singers Group.

Case study: 62

The woman in Case 62 was born in London, England (within the sound of Bow bells) around 1947. She was an only child. In her early twenties she and a friend migrated to Australia. She had always had an interest in fabric crafts and design and had watched her grandmother working as a tailor. However her mother felt that a business career would be more reliable and so she trained in office management. In Sydney she took up a position with one of the major banks. She did not marry. She did well in her career and was able to buy a flat, but over the years the notion of living in the country and pursuing her hobby of craftwork took hold. Friends came down to Tasmania and saw that the old schoolhouse at Garden Island Creek was for sale. The woman came down and looked at several properties but then made an offer for the schoolhouse. She sold her flat in Sydney and moved to the Channel twenty years ago (early 1990s?). She obtained work with a firm in Hobart and commuted there by car four days a week to work, leaving one day free for craft. She later moved to another firm but always worked part-time.

The schoolhouse was built in 1885 and stands on an acre of ground. The woman has studied its history, learning from neighbours. Some of the original features are in place and the original lay-out is quite clear. The rooms which were accommodation for the teacher are still in use and the living room and kitchen are where the school room once was. There was a large saw mill across the road and the owners donated the ground for the school. The creek was dredged in those days so that a substantial jetty served the saw mill and steamers and barquentines could pull up there to load timber from the mill. To look at the muddy creek today it would be very hard to envisage the busy scene in photographs from the late 19th century.

The woman is now retired from work and continues to make sewn and knitted goods which are of a high quality and finish and which she sells at craft markets and fairs. We looked at the list of skills which women earlier in the twentieth century would have acquired and she is confident that she could undertake most of them. She cuts wood and has felled trees, she has kept chickens, she bakes bread and makes jam, she knits and sews, she has ridden horses, knows about car maintenance, she gardens, has cooked on open fires in camps, still washes some things in the concrete wash troughs that are in the schoolhouse. She could certainly run a shop or post office and keep accounts. Altogether, though she was born half a world away, this woman could probably have adapted well to life in a much earlier Garden Island Creek.

When she came to Garden Island Creek she went to CWA meetings and joined the organisation. She served as president for Garden Island Creek CWA. They held their meetings in what was laughingly termed "the hut" but which was officially called "the Hall". The CWA has rules and regulations about the conduct of meetings which the group adhered to as best they could, but it was more a friendship group than a formal organisation. The group has since disbanded but remain friends and she still has associations with the CWA as a craft judge in competitions. From her I learned of the daffodil fairs which were held in Cygnet through the CWA.

The story is a moving one. After the 1967 February bushfires, which burned most of the buildings at Garden Island Creek with the exception of the schoolhouse, the land was black and ruined. The tragedy had scarred the whole neighbourhood. By the end of winter, however, the shoots of daffodil bulbs were poking up through the ashes and the daffodils flowered amidst the blackened ruins of gardens. So the daffodil fair was held to remember what happened and the fresh hope the flowers brought. As far as I know this no longer happens in Cygnet which seems a pity because the symbolism is strong. Perhaps people are still trying to forget what happened forty years ago.

This woman is a close friend of the subject of Case 69 whom I know from living on the Channel. I had intended to track her down for this study and have done so.

Case study: 63

The woman in Case 63 was born in Hobart (probably around the later 1930s or early 1940s). She was an only child. Her grandmother and grandfather had orchards at Lymington near Cygnet. Her grandmother was born in the Channel district around 1850. This lady was one of thirteen children.

When the woman in Case 63 was a child she contracted TB, first in her lungs and later in her spine. She spent a period of time at Winfield House in Hobart which was a sanatorium. The TB patients were housed in wards which allowed for lots of fresh air as this was the only known way to treat the disease. Polio patients and cerebral palsy patients were also in the hospital and mixed with the TB patients. At first she was held in isolation in a small room of her own which looked out onto a car park. This was her only amusement, watching the cars. When the disease appeared in her spine she underwent a bone graft. This was just at the end of the war. Two bones from another person's spine were inserted to replace diseased vertebrae. She remembers being in a "turning cage"-- a cage like structure that fitted over her bed. The staff would place pillows on her stomach and then the contraption was inverted. She remembers the process as being very painful. She notes that while there were medical treatments by then, there was no psychological help to deal with the trauma.

Because of this medical history she missed a great deal of schooling as she was kept relatively isolated at her grandparent's home at Lymington. She had private tutorials but says her education had big patches missing which she has since worked to remedy. However she went on to work as an infant teacher in Huonville. She went to Melbourne to do training and came back to teach in special schools. The children she worked with there led to an interest in social work and she moved into child welfare.

She was involved in court work and in adoptions for three or four years. She developed kidney trouble but she was intending to marry anyway so she left to be at home. She had two sons. When the youngest went to high school she returned to teaching in the 1980s. She worked with infants and Years 3 and 4 and also was Religious Co-Ordinator for the school for thirteen years. She thoroughly enjoyed the work in a small Catholic school, working on a very tight budget because Catholic schools are in the private system and funding was tight. She enjoyed the Religious Education side of her work as this involved liaison with parents and clergy.

Her husband retired and they wanted to spend time together so she followed him into retirement. They bought the old family home in Middleton twelve years ago when it was practically derelict and her husband and a friend have restored the house. They found when they arrived that the community was still suffering mentally in the aftermath of the 1967 fires. It had never recovered from the devastation. In addition, Britain joining the Common market and the Suez crisis brought hardship to the orchard industry. Some farmers had their apple crop stuck on ships stranded in the Suez Canal. There was also a quota set for dairy farmers by the Government which many could not reach and they moved away as well.

However new families had been moving in and brought new ideas, not all of which were accepted by the older residents. Some people were very comfortable with things as they were and resisted change. She has taken a leading role in the local community organisation. In that role there has been a lot of compromise and negotiation. The fortieth anniversary of the '67 fires brought the community together to build a memorial and to have past residents return to dedicate this. Since then they have worked to restore the old honour boards from WWI and the Boer War, which were burned, to their place in the community centre. They have had several reunions though the families who lived through the bushfires are getting older now. Lately they unveiled a plaque to members of the Charlton family who had large orchards.

Case study: 64

The woman in Case 64 was born in 1949, in the Bowmont hospital in Franklin. The family lived at one time at Garden Island Creek. She was one of a family of five. They moved to Charlotte Cove at the very foot of the Channel where her eldest brother was born. He became ill with rheumatic fever. The roads down there were unsealed until about 40 years ago. She thinks her father kept the family together. He earned a living working on the roads. Her mother had no education and was 21 when she had her first child. The woman attended Cygnet Area School. She won a scholarship to Secretarial School in Hobart. She boarded in Hobart at the Salvation Army Hostel for a year. Her first job was in Cygnet working for the Cygnet Canning Company in their office and at weekends she worked in the cannery itself, earning more doing this than she did in secretarial work.

When the woman was 19 the family moved to Montrose on the outskirts of Hobart. She met and married a second cousin from Gordon and they moved back to Middleton to live on fifteen acres of land. She had two sons. Her first husband was German on his father's side. Their home in Middleton was near the shop. He was the milkman for a local company in the area and delivered milk all over the Huon. By the time the family lived in Middleton the bush fires had gone through and they could no longer make a living on fifteen acres of ground. Her husband developed cancer and she nursed him though this final illness with help from nursing staff who came in daily. He died in 1996. In 2000 she married again. Her second husband died in 2006.

Her father served in the army and the woman was very fond of him and dreaded losing him all her adult life. She seems to have been very attached to her father but fought with her mother. She felt her mother manipulated her father and was an unfeeling woman who made her do a lot of housework. She says her childhood was boring having so much demanded of her. Her mother was an excellent nurse, however, caring for those around her through mumps, measles etc.

The Clements family had the first saw mill in Garden Island Creek and the woman's grandparents bought the house from them. Her husband's father used to ride his bike into Cygnet. His grandfather would ride from Garden Island Creek to Franklin for dances.

The roads in the area were sealed around 1960. There was a bus from Deep Bay to Hobart in the days when there were no sealed roads. The trip took two hours with a stop at Gordon where there was a shop.

In her second marriage she lived at Flowerpot. By her reckoning there were houses there which escaped the 1967 fires. She now has a house in Margate in a new development, but when we spoke she was living with her new partner in his house which overlooks all the new buildings now, but once looked down onto orchards on the flood plain. The woman regrets that secretarial work was her only choice when she left school. She loves gardening and would have liked to do nursery garden work.

Case study: 65

The woman in Case 65 is the youngest I have spoken to. She is under 40 years old, lives in a small town in the Huon Valley with her partner and two sons by her first marriage. She was born in Queensland and went to school there. She had one brother and two sisters. They had a three bedroomed house in Queensland. She attended State schools in Queensland. The High School took children from all the smaller feeder primary schools. She was 18 when she left school. She attended University for two years but did not complete the course.

The house the family live in at present is a two bedroomed cottage on the outskirts of the town. She has worked in the past but is out of work at the present and is looking for part time work. Her interests lie in gardening and working with plants. She would also be interested in doing Youth Work. At present she has a productive garden and supplies vegetables to local restaurants in her locality. This means she is at home most of the time and does not have to travel to work as she did in the past.

The woman sees the town she lives in as a very vibrant community with classes in Yoga and festivals throughout the year. She remembers as a child that all the small towns in Queensland had dances and that the kids would fall asleep on the benches around the hall. This would have been in the 1970s and 80s. Since she has lived in her present home the town has become much busier with many more people and increased traffic.

The threat of bushfires is the reality in the district and this year (2013) has seen destruction at Dunally, reminding people of what happened here in 1967. The woman points out, however, that warning systems now in place on the radio, with 'phone messages and the availability of the site at www.fire.tas.gov.au means that you can now access pretty well instantaneous information about the threat of fire, where in the past you would see smoke and not know what was happening. Her family have experienced minor flooding where they have lived here but no serious natural disasters. Despite the "news cycle" on TV and the awareness of events overseas she does not feel threatened in any way by events abroad.

Case study: 66

This participant was born in northern Tasmania. She is in the 40 to 60 age group. She has two brothers. She has two children.
Her home in childhood was a two storey brick house. The family had electricity connected, a 'fridge, TV, record player, and a twin tub washing machine. As a child she just generally helped around the home.
The participant now lives near to a small town in the Huon Valley. As a child she moved house many times. The house she lives in now is smaller than the one she grew up in. She lived as a child in the country and then in the town and now she lives by the sea.
She started her schooling at a local District School then moved to High School. Then she attended another High School, followed by Technical College and then went on to the University of Tasmania. The District School went from Grade 1 to Grade 10. It was a small school taking children from the age of six to the age of 15/16. The woman left school at 16 but then went on to take a University Degree.
Her local community has a very active social calendar and she attends Arts and Music events. The community is a lot busier now and more cosmopolitan with people coming to live here from the mainland and from overseas. There is more emphasis on tourism. She has been working in her present occupation for 6 years. She has to travel to reach work (a journey of around twenty minutes by car). There have been no impacts from natural disasters in the time she has lived in the area.
When she was a child the apple orchards on the property were removed and replaced with other agricultural practices. She now has a vegetable and fruit garden at her home.

She believes that the local fish farms affect recreational fishing in the area in which she lives. She has also seen more forestry activity in the area. Her present workplace has equal opportunities for men and women, so while she takes an interest in women's issues they do not affect her at work. Her response to questions shows that she takes a keen interest in environmental issues such as conservation of forests for biodiversity, sustainable agriculture, organic growing, and uses home or locally grown food wherever possible.

Case study: 67

The participant was born in the UK and immigrated to mainland Australia at the age of fifteen with her family. She is in the age group 40 to 60 years old. The family lived in a three bedroom house before leaving for Australia. They had the usual appliances—washing machine, TV, record player, radio, vacuum etc. The first house they lived in in Australia was a rented bungalow with three bedrooms. As a child she did help a little in the house but it was not insisted upon. She has two siblings and has two children of her own. At present she lives near to Oyster Cove on a country property which is well off the main road. As a child she moved house a number of times with her family and then they made the quantum leap of coming to Australia. She attended two Primary schools near to where she was then living as child (ages 5 to 11+).

She then moved to a Secondary School in the UK till she was fifteen and left the country. On coming to Australia she attended one High School in Year 11, then moved house and completed Year 12 at a second High School. She left school at 17 and went directly to University where she completed two degrees. Between studying for those degrees she spent time in the north of Western Australia. She moved to Tasmania several years ago from inter-state.

The local community has a busy social programme with school events, occasional movie nights, bush dances, festivals, sports commitments etc. She attends many of these and also events in Hobart. In the years that she has lived in this area the community has grown and she has many friends who have come to live in the area as her family has.

The woman works in Hobart. She has held her current post for nine years. She works with young people. She and her husband commute to Hobart daily, alternately taking bus and car to allow for school drop-off and pick-up. The journey takes between fifty minutes and an hour by car depending on traffic. They live in a bush setting so fire is a hazard but there have been no fires near in the time she has lived here.

The property is on several acres. They keep chickens, but the pressure of other commitments does not leave much time for gardening or other land use. They hope to make more use of the land in future years. They have not experienced any land use changes in the time they have lived here.

She takes a keen interest in women's issues and environmental issues. She works in the public service so employment issues are well regulated.

Case study: 68

The participant was born in Sydney and moved as a young child with her family to live in the Cygnet Area. They were seeking a more rural lifestyle. In fact she lives at present in the same road as did the woman in Case 4 many years ago. She is aged between 20 and 40 years.

She was part of a family of five children and has two brothers and two sisters. She has one child of her own. The home she lived in as a child had electricity connected with a slow combustion stove for hot water and this was supplemented by a solar panel when there was enough sunshine. She performed what she describes as age-appropriate tasks around the home as a child, such as washing up, taking clothes in from the washing line, bringing in wood, tidying her shared bedroom and caring for younger children.

She describes living in many country areas, mostly in Tasmania. She studied at University in Hobart , obtained two bachelor degrees and entered the teaching profession. She moved regularly in her work as a teacher. She has moved back to her present location to bring up her young son.

As a child she attended a local school, which had around 300 pupils, which took students from the age of six or seven to 16 in yr. 10. She also attended a school in NSW with around 400 pupils which took students during their Primary Schooling. She moved around with her family and attended one small school in Victoria with 28 students and another rural school in Tasmania which had 250 students. Following her Year 10 education she moved to study at a Year 11/12 College in Hobart. She left school at the age of 18 and moved to University where she completed her two degrees.

The participant enjoys living in a rural area as she maintains a better social life there than in the city. There is so much to do for families. Her child can take part in Kinder Gym, in the Launching into Learning program, attends Playgroup and has story time sessions in the local library.

In the years in which she has lived in the area she has seen great changes with many more cafes and many more tourists coming into the area. There is a marked demographic difference now as compared to the years in which she was growing up. Earlier there was a "huge" divide between what might be described then as the "hippy" community and those who had been born and grown up in the area. Now the spectrum of inhabitants is wider and there is usually more harmony.

The participant has spent twelve years teaching. She can walk to work or takes the car on occasion. The journey is a short one of around five minutes.

She has not experienced any natural disasters while living in the area. She cultivates a garden with apple trees, carrots, zucchini, lettuce and rhubarb. Her family lived on a property she describes as a Post War block. The orchard which was there was grubbed out because the wet conditions did not suit the apple trees.

The participant has active political interests and is a member of the teaching union. She acknowledges that there is a wealth of information now about world events and tries to keep up to date with major events while avoiding "violent" gossip and "non-news" news. She uses the Internet to filter stories.

Her family's move to Tasmania was triggered by a desire for an "alternative" lifestyle. They lived a more-or-less self-sufficient lifestyle. Their political views would have leaned more to the left than the right. At one stage they took legal action over a plan to plant plantation trees above a creek which provided their water supply. They won this action. This has been the only direct concern she has had over environmental issues but her political leanings might bias her towards environmental concerns.

Case study: 69

This woman was one of seven children. She is the great-great-granddaughter of Fanny Cochrane Smith, an Aboriginal woman who had lived at Oyster Cove and married an ex-convict from England, William Smith. They had eleven children so have numerous descendants. The woman's family still lived in the same neighbourhood. It would seem her childhood was not particularly happy. Her parents, in her words, drank too much and had friends who visited who shared this habit of alcohol abuse. She seems to have had a much better relationship with other Aunties, relatives and friends who treated her more kindly.

The woman in this case worked around the family property in her childhood. In particular she had tasks with the poultry. In her childhood the house did not have running water until a local dam was built, but they had electricity, a washing machine and a telephone. Her father was injured in an accident and this added to the family difficulties. Her parent's marriage was opposed by her mother's family, so while she knew her grandmother, her grandfather would not recognise her, though he lived nearby. She spent a lot of time with friends who also lived on a property adjacent to her home and considers herself a part of their family.

She went to a Catholic school in a nearby town and she says she owes a great deal to the nuns, most of whom were very kind. She remembers being at school on the day of the 1967 bushfires (see Chapter 9). Late in her education she had to move to the local State school but she says she was treated with kindness there.

On leaving school she had an ambition to join the police or the armed services, but her family mocked the idea. She went to work in a store in the town, boarding there with local families. After some time she moved to work in another local business. She married a local farmer and has three sons, who now run the farm. She lived on that farm for over thirty years. Now she and her husband are retired and have moved further up the Channel. She misses her home down at the farm. Her sons have children of their own and she helps her daughter's-in-law with the children as they work part-time. She has made a career for herself in a branch of what might be described as community service and is very successful in this.

Case study: 70

The woman in this Case was one of five children. Her husband was one of ten children.

She was the daughter of an orchard owner. As a child she started school at seven and left at 14. She was offered the chance to stay on at school but refused and went to work in the orchards instead at the age of 14. It was pretty well year-long work between picking and then pruning and hoeing around the trees. She would have liked to be a teacher, but she would have had to go away to train and she was engaged. She compensated by teaching in Sunday School. Her fiancée didn't want her to go away as he thought the engagement would have lapsed, so she stayed at home. There were dances at Geeveston and Wattle Grove across the river. Also there were dances on the apple ships at Port Huon. The young couple were engaged for ten years. Her husband, as he became, was a farmer and orchard owner and they had three children, though one died in infancy. They settled near Castle Forbes Bay.

Her husband owned a farming and orchard property of around 24 acres. As her children grew up the house had electricity, but the woman still used the copper for washing. She had twin sinks with a small wringer clamped between them (like the one in the photo on page 20). Her daughter remembers the Home Arts teacher at High School assuming that all the girls would have washing machines at home and she sat very quietly at the back of the class not wanting to say "Well, actually, no."

When they eventually got a washing machine it had an electric wringer attached. The woman's husband died in 1958 and she took over the running of the property. She had to learn to drive at that time. At the time of the bushfires in 1967 she defended her property single handed. Her home was saved.

Case study: 71

The woman in Case 71 was born in 1956 at the Bowmont Hospital in Franklin and grew up near Castle Forbes Bay. She is the daughter of the woman in Case 70. She was one of three children (one sibling died in infancy). Her father died when she was very young. She grew up with her mother running the family property.

She went to primary school in Franklin, then Huonville High and then went on to Hobart College, travelling daily from Castle Forbes Bay. In her teens there were dances at Huonville Town Hall and there were live shows and movies at the Palais theatre in Franklin. There were still ships coming into Port Huon to collect apples when she was growing up. When she was at school, Franklin was a hive of activity. The family did all their shopping there. There was a butcher's shop, a chemist, an electrical goods shop, a grocer, which also sold household goods and hardware, a milk bar, a drapery/shoe shop, a fish and chips shop and bread was delivered from the bakery twice a week. Over time businesses relocated to Huonville and Franklin became much less busy.

The woman remembers the 1967 bush fires well. The buses came to the school and took the children home. She says the hills were ablaze. Her mother had struggled all day to keep the house hosed down, but then they were told to evacuate. They drove to friends near Franklin. Her mother grabbed papers, photos and jewellery and told the girls to get what they wanted to take. The woman wanted to take her piano but that was impractical! Her grandparents' two storey timber house was lost probably because it had large pine trees near it, but her own home survived. Her mother sold their property in the years just before the apple industry collapsed.

She left school at seventeen and sat the entrance exams for the Public Service. She found work in that service and worked there for ten years till 1984. She met her husband in Hobart and married at eighteen in 1974. They lived in Hobart for a while then purchased land near Judbury in 1978 with plans to build their own home. They moved there in 1980. At first they had built a well-constructed wooden shed and lived there with a wood fired stove for heating and cooking and a generator to supply electricity until they got power connected after about 18 months. The woman jokes that when the generator ran out of fuel in the evenings they just packed up and went to bed. Then when it was refuelled in the morning everything cranked up again. Eventually in 1987 they completed their house just before their first child was born. She has three children. Her husband was a tradesman but they now manage their property and he does voluntary work. He suffers from R.S.I. as a result of his working life.

The couple take an interest in world events through radio and television news though the woman monitors and filters what she sees. They are both strongly supportive of environmental issues and this commitment has been costly at times in a small community heavily dependent on the timber industry. Sometimes they have felt ostracised by neighbours and local tradesmen. The small community they live in is spread out over a large area with about 300 people resident there. The local school closed just as their eldest son was approaching school age.

Case study: 72

The woman in Case 72 was born in Cygnet in the 1960s at what was then known as the Cygnet Health Centre. Her father owned an orchard and dairy property near to Cygnet. He built the weatherboard house on the property. She was one of a family of six children. With five siblings in the house she had to share the sleep-out with her brother. A curtain partitioned the space. The woman had to help around the house at weekends but otherwise had few demands made on her. She remembers that her brother had to milk the cow in the mornings and was always rushing to get to school. She started school aged six. Her husband was also one of a large family and was required to work hard on his parent's property.

Her father held a prominent position on the Cygnet Council. He died after illness when he was in his forties. There is some suggestion that the illness he suffered was caused by exposure to chemicals during war service in the Pacific. Before his death he made arrangements that his wife and children would move to live with her sister who ran an orchard across the Huon River. His widow moved the family and she and her sister raised them. Ancestors of the family had come from Scotland and had established a shipwright's business on the river.

The move meant that the woman then had to share a double bed with her sister, which did not please her. Her mother was left with a small widow's pension so money was scarce. When she changed schools as part of the move her mother could not afford the cost of new school uniforms so she had to wear her old one. She felt it really made her stand out as a "new kid". She remembers the day of the 1967 bushfires vividly. The school buses took the children home. Her aunt and mother had apple sacks soaking in the pond and the whole family used these to beat out spot fires around the house where burning embers were falling. It was late into the night before they were able to go to bed.

She left school when she was eighteen, then did a year's course in child care. She married a farmer and orchard grower and they have three children. Much later she enrolled at University to complete a Bachelor's degree in Fine Arts. She was successful and graduated with distinction, but she found the lecturers unsympathetic and unhelpful. Of the seven women who enrolled with her she was the only one to complete the degree. Others accepted a lesser qualification.

She and her husband live in the upper Huon Valley in a rural setting. Her husband has recently retired from work. He sold the property several years ago but stayed on to manage it for the new owners. When the apple industry collapsed he diversified into dairy farming. At one time the woman reckons there would have been around 137 dairy farms in Southern Tasmania, but that industry met with difficulties in relation to milk price and contracts. She cites, as an example of how things were, the fact that some farmers were emptying vats of milk down the drain. She notes that, while the farmers were struggling with losses, the unionised workers in the factory were still on full pay. There are now few, if any, dairy farms in the district. Her husband changed to cherry growing then sold the property. She says ruefully that the only time they made real money was the day they sold the farm.

There is no small village where she lives, only scattered properties, so there is not a great deal of community life, though there may have been more in the past. The woman does voluntary work in Hobart which she really enjoys and gardens and works around the property.

She describes her aunt who took the family in, (Case 29), as a woman of great skill and determination. She also describes her grandmother as a "suffragette" who travelled with the local midwife all around the Cygnet district delivering babies. She has a philosophy that as a society we are too ready to reach out and demand help. "People need to accept ownership of their problems, for example health issues, and try to address them. Perhaps the government should subsidise healthy food? We should be responsible for ourselves."

Case study: 73

The woman in this Case study was born in 1938 in a hospital in Hobart. Her parents lived in Gordon and she has lived all her life in the area. Her father had a scallop fishing boat and a processing shed in addition to berry fields and a small orchard. At one time when she was a child there were twenty to thirty scallop boats tied up at Gordon beside the oval and ten scallop processing sheds all around the shore there. Two sheds are still there, one of which now belongs to her. It's empty and the floor floods on a high tide, but they hold parties down there. The jetty was much bigger with "wings" at the sides.

Her father also had a portable sawmill and he sold that engine to the Hydro. She worked in the scallop sheds along with four to six other women and then when the scallop season was over went fruit and berry picking. The advent of the Sputnick dredge, invented at Gordon, stripped the scallop beds and the industry collapsed. There is still a scallop splitting industry at Margate but skilled splitters are in short supply and she has offered to help out if they need her.

She was one of three children. She describes Gordon before the 1967 bushfires. The village had two shops, a post office, a church, a hall, a school (the school house is still there though the school was lost along with most of the other amenities in the fires). In her view it was a close knit community where everybody helped and shared—if you had a good catch of fish you would give surplus to your neighbours, same with the vegetable crop. Nowadays while people still take pride in their place there are a lot of strangers who don't seem to relate to the traditions of the community—for example in the past if there was an event such as a dance everyone would pitch in to organise it—now younger people are all working, women included, and when the older people who are organising now pass away, who will do things like the Middleton Fair? As a child she and her brothers made their own fun, building trucks out of flat bits of packing case and riding these around the yard. They also had a sledge and would career down the hill. "I demanded to sit on the back to be safe, but the sledge hit a bush and we all went up in the air and when we landed I was on the bottom with my brothers and the sledge on top of me."

The woman married in 1957 and comments that when they got married they had the basic furniture and no luxuries—which contrasts to what happens nowadays with gift lists and the cost of weddings. They had six children. Their first car was an old Austin with a canvas hood. Her husband also had a scallop boat so she worked alongside him in the sheds. Sometimes the boats would come in late in the evening and you had to work through as much of the catch as you could into the night then finish off in the morning. The trucks would come to take the catch to Hobart or further up the Channel. The scallop season lasted three months. Her husband had retired but still had his boat and was tragically killed in a boating accident last year. They had moved from Gordon to a house beyond Middleton only four years before the accident. She says that despite the fact that she thinks everybody is more selfish these days and there is not the same sense of community, she was amazed and humbled by the amount of help which she was given following her husband's loss and in the days when his body had not been recovered.

She would love to go back to Gordon but they sold their home there before the move. All her children still live in the Channel area. She has ten grandchildren and ten great-grandchildren.

When she was young they had electricity connected to the house. Her Mum still washed often in the copper, though her husband did buy her a washing machine. Monday was a day set aside for washing. Her mother worked in the scallop shed, splitting scallops. She didn't like the work but her husband was running the business and she had to help. The woman was taken down to the shed when she was about six and used to stand on a box and watch and learn. You could earn very good money scallop splitting and also fruit packing.

As a child she spent 12 months living at Lena Valley when her grandmother was ill. Apart from that school year she attended Gordon school, then moved to Middleton school and then to Woodbridge. She left school before her fifteenth birthday because her mother had to go to care for her mother and she stepped in at home to look after her brothers and her father. Her father's mother died when she was in her twenties.

Her first employment was in Hobart as a shop assistant (she lived with her aunt) but she didn't like being there and was glad to come back home. She then got work at the Post Office in Middleton working the telephone exchange there before she married.

She vividly remembers the 1967 bushfires. The day was her youngest child's birthday and they were planning a birthday tea when the older four children came home from school at Woodbridge. Her mother and father lived just down the road and her mother usually baked a birthday cake, but because it was so hot they decided to buy a sponge and ice it. So the woman set off with the two little girls and the pusher to the local shop, bought the sponge and took it back to her mother's house. The wind was howling. Then the fires came. Her husband had just ploughed around her house so the ground was bare and there was nothing to burn, but fire balls were blowing across the Channel from Bruny island. She had made a little pond over a spring for a duck she had and she and the children sat in this. The smoke was so thick she says you could not see your hands in front of your face. Her house was safe but her mother's house burned. Both her husband and father were away from home so her mother came and sheltered with her. The birthday sponge burned with her mother's house and the older children had to stay with friends in Woodbridge as they could not get home. She says that it was weird that her mother's washing was still hanging on the line, covered in ash, though the house was gone. After the fires the community was decimated. There was nothing left to allow them to make a living and many had to move. The whole place became very quiet.

Nowadays she lives alone although her family are nearby. She loves knitting, has a computer but doesn't know how to use it, doesn't watch much TV but gardens and looks after her property.

Case study: 74

I met with these two women who are sisters together to hear a little of their story. They were born around 1950 at Nichols Rivulet just round the corner from the woman in Case 69 and were good friends to her. Their father had an orchard. They were part of a family of twelve children, five girls and seven boys. They went to the Area School in Cygnet. They were keen netball players and were eligible to play for the district because they attended the Area school. They played matches in Hobart.

The younger woman remembers being so nervous the first time she had to go to play there—getting a bus from Huonville. It seemed such a long way from home. These girls are described in the story of Case 69's adolescence, getting ready for dances in Cygnet. They insist these were real dances (not discos) with Progressive Barn dances and Pride of Erin Waltzes (you got to meet all the boys in the progressive dances!). The elder woman moved on to play netball at senior level. Both married, though the younger is no longer with her husband and has had two more partners. All the sisters keep in close touch.

Case study: 75

The woman in Case Study 75 was born in Melbourne in 1956. She provided me with a vivid written account of her life.

She is one of a family of six children and has a twin sister. In discussion, she points out that large families were very common in the district she grew up in. The family are Presbyterian so religious teaching was not the impetus. Rather, after the war, the phrase "populate or perish" was widely used in Australia—so everyone populated. She notes that nowadays there is some head-shaking if a family has as many as four children! She has three sons.

Growing up in Melbourne in the 1950s she met conditions which would seem strange there today. The family lived on the outskirts of the city in an area which still had paddocks and fruit orchards further out. She would describe her family as "struggling middle class". Her father worked full-time and sometimes at weekends. Her mother was kept busy at home raising the six children. Most mothers in the neighbourhood were "stay at home Mums". A lack of transport and six children meant the family lived a fairly quiet life. Social events in her community centred round the Churches. The Church provided Sunday School and youth group. In addition there were Church netball leagues in which she was a keen player. Sundays might also include a drive to visit relatives or a trip to the beach. All the children in the neighbourhood would play on the street after school and at weekends. They skipped, played ball games, hop-scotch, cowboys and Indians or, for the girls, took their dolls for a walk. One of the neighbouring houses had a TV and another had a tree house for games. The children learned to be independent and self-sufficient, but had roster responsibilities at home which had to be fulfilled. These rosters included dish-washing, cleaning the bed rooms and the bathroom and making lunches.

As a child she remembers that "the dunny man" still came around to empty the drop toilets. When her school installed new "modern" toilets it was a highlight of the school year. The milkman still came around with his horse and cart, as did the baker in his small Morris van. She thinks she would have been about eight years old when this way of life began to end.

The highlights of the family year were Christmas and birthdays. In the school holidays the family packed up and went camping for a month. On these holidays she learned to love the bush and being by the sea. The outdoor life was what she enjoyed.

She attended a local Primary school, then went on to High School. She remembers that in the "prep" year they still worked with chalk and slates.

By the time the woman reached her teen-age years she had become disillusioned with her life in the suburbs. She still enjoyed playing netball, but nothing much else was of interest.

She was quiet, serious and very studious and spent much of her time studying. When she went to work in the city she found that her workmates would go shopping in lunch breaks while she would sit alone with a much-enjoyed picnic by the Yarra River. This feeling of disconnection was a driving force behind later decisions to move to the country.

She was able to attend university in Melbourne "because Goff Whitlam brought in free University places". If this had not happened her family could not have sent her to study there. She completed a BA degree majoring in psychology and sociology at Swinburne in 1977 but found it hard to find work in the field. At school she had enjoyed "keyboard" studies, so she did find work in the secretarial field as a typist, receptionist, clerk and terminal operator.

Her first visit to Tasmania was as part of a Church trip to walk at Cradle Mountain and Dove Lake. Later she toured all around the State on a motor bike and loved the countryside. Friends with whom she was travelling knew a family at Garden Island Creek and this was her introduction to the area around Cygnet. She returned to Melbourne and lived with her partner whom she later married. When I asked whether her parents were shocked by this arrangement she pointed out that her older sister had broken this taboo already. Her parents were much more distressed about her decision to move "so far away" to Tasmania. The young couple had friends who were contemplating moving to St. Helens in the north of the State but she told them how lovely Cygnet was and they moved there.

She and her partner worked for a time to save up to buy land down in Tasmania to allow them to move away from the city. Land in Tasmania was very cheap in the 1970s. The woman laughs when she remembers that selling a Morris Minor van for $100.00 could buy ten acres of land with the proceeds. Eventually the couple bought 50 acres of land for $5,000.00 in 1978. She remembers the first time she saw their land on a misty day. The mist seemed like a metaphor for their new lives, with so much hidden and about to be revealed. They arrived from Melbourne with two cars, pitched a tent on the land and began work. They had no Hydro power, but connected to the car battery to obtain 12 volt lighting. A portable black and white TV occasionally provided entertainment. She says they, in contrast to their city peers, stepped back in time to using hand held appliances, cooking on an open fire and sewing on an old treadle machine. They were able to re-capture old ideas and re-invent ways of looking at life, exploring the environment, herbal medicines, wholefood cooking and making use of recycling.

They built a very basic home on the block as a workshop/house. They used a pole construction (the poles were stringy bark eucalypts), clad the house in wattle and daub and vertical boards from the local sawmill. They also built a studio with a stud frame on rock foundations. Plywood to clad and line the studio was sourced from cases which once held cocoa butter for the Cadbury's chocolate factory in Hobart. The inner walls were then lined with hessian. Other recycled goods were sourced from what, at that time, was an open tip site.

They cut access roads and got to know others who were seeking a similar lifestyle. The woman learned to love using her hands in practical tasks. She found it a revelation that she could create things around her which would last and the discipline she had acquired studying paid off as she worked to complete tasks. New skills could be learned locally.

Throughout this period she feels that the locals were puzzled and disapproving of these city born newcomers who were living an alternative life-style. The woman says that one shopkeeper hardly spoke to her for ten years until she was pregnant and had become more accepted. The older people they met, especially the older men, were more supportive. They had at one time lived in similar circumstances, bringing up their families in the bush. The townsfolk didn't see the work that was done, clearing land, building gardens, making drains, wood-cutting and splitting, fencing, fixing cars and often in such cold and wet conditions that the work had to be completed as quickly as possible. The general preconception was that the newcomers lived on the "dole" and hung around doing nothing—very far from the hard work which was the truth.

By 1979 the woman had completed a Diploma in Primary teaching at the University of Tasmania. She and her partner had established a business making furniture, craft articles from local wood and musical instruments. As was often the case in families who had ventured down to live in the Tasmanian bush, the woman became the family breadwinner to allow the men to build, to work on the properties and to establish careers. She used her teaching skills and secretarial skills to obtain work teaching keyboard studies in schools. She was also required to teach shorthand, which she hadn't studied. She enrolled in shorthand classes in Hobart. Her work was at a school in the Derwent Valley, so she would go up to Hobart for evening classes, spend the night there then go north west. She would teach for two days, staying locally, then return to Hobart for a further evening class before returning home. Later she found work nearer to home. She taught for three years, marrying during this time. Her first child was born in 1983 at Franklin Hospital. Both her later children were born in home births.

At times she says she felt lonely and cut off, living "up on the hill". She had only been 22 years of age when she arrived and was younger than many of the others who were sharing this life-style. Their diverse backgrounds were interesting and thought provoking. The group was small and in time they constituted an extended family. They would socialise together with all the children coming along. They formed a supportive and active friendship network and formed a netball team which took part in local competitions. She says this was the best thing they could have done as they all made friends locally through sport. There were a few misunderstandings. A pick-me-up remedy from alternative medicine involves infusing flower petals in water or sometimes, for a longer preserved version, in brandy. The women in her team knew and used this remedy. They would take a quick sip of this at half-time in matches and soon found that their opponents believed they were taking swigs of raw brandy and disapproved of this. They introduced other teams to the medicinal benefits of the pick-me-up and all was peaceful again.

She says that despite local preconceptions most of them were hard working, well-educated, a bit scruffy in dress, but clean and keen to be seen as part of the community. When the children were born she became a lot more involved with the local Cygnet people. She loved the locals close ties to family and land; their industrious and down-to earth nature. She feels that she belongs here. She lived on her land with her partner and children for sixteen years.

For practical reasons, however, they have lived in rental properties throughout their years in Tasmania. When their sons became of age to attend High School they moved for a number of years to live in Taroona before coming back to Cygnet. She has still kept her close ties with their property using it as a family bush shack or just somewhere where she can go and sit quietly or get stuck into some tasks. She felt those years in the bush shaped her showing her her own strengths and boosting her confidence.

After her children were born she was "a home Mum" for a while. Her husband now makes musical instruments and the woman helps make the harps and keeps the books. The use of the internet has enabled them to build up this business.

She liked to work outdoors when she could so she took up organic orchard work part-time when her children started school. She still works there today. She loves working there through the seasons, driving locally to the orchard and the flexibility of the hours has kept her there.

In addition, in her years living in Tasmania she has taken part in many community groups. She was part of the blockade on the Franklin River and a member of the Huon Protection Group and the Cygnet Arts Council. She became involved in drama in the 80s through the Cygnet Performing Arts Group (CPAG) and the Black Stump Theatre at Mt.Cygnet . The building of the stage was a group volunteer effort that she became involved with. Later she worked as one of the organisers for the Hobart Fringe Festival. Her years in drama involved youth drama, stage managing, working back stage, writing material, performing and directing. She is a keen participator in sport and a volunteer at the Cygnet Living History Museum.

Appendix 2: Women's war effort in World War I

From "The Daily Mail" 233 Regents Street, London. Around 1914 (the newspaper cutting does not give a specific date).

What Women Can Do. *The way to help our soldiers and sailors. British Red Cross patterns.*

The enthusiasm of the women who are willing and eager to help our soldiers and sailors by making garments for them is very good to realise. Today's patterns are for pyjamas and "the helpless case" shirt, which to be effective and comfortable should be very carefully cut out and made. It is not necessary to say that those qualifications apply to all garments intended for the purpose in view, and to the end that they be skilfully cut, by the aid of good patterns, experts in the art of cutting should be "told off" for that purpose. Others will sew and put on buttons and so forth.

One woman declares that she and her band of dedicated helpers are not going to have working parties " because the tea part of them takes too long"- She is calling a morning meeting for cutting out the garments and wrapping them up in separate bundles to be sent for by those who are ready to sew.

Each parcel will have to be back at her house within a specified time, with the garments ready to be packed off to the British Red Cross Society, Devonshire House, Piccadilly, W1 and the parcels that contain the goods, may I remind all concerned, must have the contents described outside and inside as well.

The above article is taken from a scrapbook compiled of newspaper cuttings from Britain in the early years of the twentieth century. The scrapbook is in my possession, having been purchased many years ago in an antique shop. I expect that the sewing groups in the Huon and Channel (at Glen Huon for example) would have followed similar Red Cross patterns and received similar detailed instructions.

Appendix 3: "Grandview" and Harry Sayer's homes prior to the fires

"Grandview"

Harry Sayer's home

Diary for February 7th. 1967

Written by Harry Sayer of Middleton (1895-1981)

This is a transcript of an account written after the fires. "Tuesday February 7th. 1967. Never to be forgotten."

The Gospel according to Harry on Feb. 7th. 1967.

On this particular morning I was up very early in fact I was up before the sun and it was very warm, the temp. being about 70degrees before the sun was up and when it came up it was like a ball of fire and I had an idea that we were in for a bad day but not as bad as it turned out to be. So I will try and give a little bit of my experience as the day went on.

Well I had my usual cup of tea and a bit of toast and that was all I had till about 6pm. Anyway when I went out to milk Julie I found it was getting very hot with a light N.W. wind and there was smoke and fire all around the hills. Well, after I had milked and aspirated and fed Jamie and the fowls I went back inside and the 'phone rang. It was Col Sayer from Hobart asking if I was alright. I said things looked pretty bad, but I thought I would be alright and that was one time I wish I had spoken my mind (as you will see as the day goes on).

Well it was now about 10am and it had got very hot, with a hot N.W.

wind. I got all the buckets and cans I could find filled them and placed them round the house as I could now see we were in for it. I could see the fire wearing down on Grandview but could do nothing about it but I was thankful that Ted Armstrong was up there.

You know there is a passage in the Bible which says there was a man sent from God whose name was John and I am going to say this I believe there was a man sent from God whose name was Ted Armstrong very seldom comes down but he was here on Feb.7th. and on his own and I don't know what I would have done without him. He got Pearl, Bill and Reg Mason down to the beach and then tried to save Grandview, the house. It is now about 11am. The heat has got terrible with the wind very strong and thick smoke everywhere. I ducked inside for a drink but did not get it as the 'phone rang and it was Col again asking how things were now and I said mate things could not look worse come down as soon as you can and bring help if you can get it we are going to be lucky to get out of this alive (well he started to come down almost at once but only got as far as the school at Woodbridge and it was about 4pm before they would let anyone go further south. But while he was waiting he twice put out a fire at the Methodist church at Woodbridge).

When I got outside again the sparks were falling as thick as snow but not quite so cooling. I started putting out fires all around the house. I had a small hand pump, but I could see I was not going to keep up with it and no chance of getting any help so I had to fight a lone battle as everyone else was doing the same but I fought on. Then I saw a fire under the back veranda roof. I got it out as I thought. Then the woodshed burst into flames but just had to let it go. Ted tried to put it out but no good he had just come down and said Grandview had gone and I don't think we can save yours to me. I said no, don't give up yet. Then the back veranda got alight again, also the front veranda. Ted said "Where is your car Uncle?" "Oh my goodness still in the garage." I ran down the heat was terrible opened the doors and all the back of the garage was alight. I got her out but we could now see it was all up and it was getting very dark.

Then I thought of my hearing aid I knew it was on the organ could not get in the back door now it was too hot went to the front, door was locked broke it open and inside was just like an oven and almost black dark. I stood for a second then in I went and got the aid, camera and banknotes which were altogether on the organ and on the way out I thought of Mother's big family Bible in another room, again I stood for a second but I went and got it and that was all but I thanked God I got out with my life. I put them in the back of the car also Roger and took the car along to the front of Mrs. L. Mason the only place where there seemed to be no fire and then went back to have a last look at the dear old house but it had all burst into flame and it was quite dark . I don't know what the time would be now as I had lost track of the day.

There were now eight buildings on fire all around us including the two Churches, Sunday School, Post Office, Public Hall and local Store. Well after the fire had beat us Ted and I we went over to keep watch at Mrs. Masons place as there was no one about, they had all gone to the beach the heat was terrible.

Ted said "I will keep watch here if you take those folk down some water". I said alright and off I started in the car. I just about got roasted passing the Hall. It was like Hell let loose and to make it worse I got caught in some wire across the road put the wind up me a bit thought it might be electric but I got out of it and came back to earth again and on I went to find Pearl, Bill and Reg it was dark with fire everywhere but I found them down by Alan Dean's jetty they all had a good drink but they were in sore distress the track that took them down to the rocks was now all ablaze which made it a track of no return and they could not get back up the stone wall. Poor Pearl she did a wonderful job. Reg was under a wet blanket by the stone wall Bill under another one by a big rock Pearl out in the water trying to keep alive. All the jetty was alight and the fire right down to the road. I said you can't stay here Pearl she said what are we going to do? Just then Alan Dean came down he said I have got to move my boat I said that's our way out bring the boat ashore and we can get the old folk into it and row them round to the sand and that is what we did with Roma Raes help. And when we got round to the sand what another sight just about all of Middleton was there. Old folk young mothers with little babies in arms some under blankets some in the water others out in boats all trying to keep cool and wondering if they would have a home to go back to. I am not ashamed to say I asked a quiet one. There were a lot of bunks to be found that night some slept in their cars on the beach (or did they) I don't think there would be much sleep.

Well there it is that is a bit of what I and all of Middleton went through on that 7th day of February 1967 and then followed the 8th with all its heartaches and thoughts of what we had lost. But cheer up we are still alive and thank God.

This account is included here with the permission of relatives of Harry Sayer. I acknowledge their help with deep gratitude.

www.ingramcontent.com/pod-product-compliance
Lightning Source LLC
Chambersburg PA
CBHW071336090426
42738CB00012B/2911